F.L.O.W.™ THE EQUITY-CENTERED COACHING FRAMEWORK

A PRACTICAL, NEURO-INCLUSIVE COACHING MODEL FOR GUIDING TEAMS TOWARD CLARITY, EQUITY, AND SUSTAINED PERFORMANCE.

DR. REBA CLARKE-WEDDERBURN

THE CHANJE COLLECTIVE PRESS

F.L.O.W.™ The Equity-Centered Coaching Framework

By Dr. Reba Clarke-Wedderburn

Published by The Chanje Collective Press™

www.chanjecollective.com/press

Copyright © 2025 Dr. Reba Clarke-Wedderburn

All rights reserved. No part of this publication may be reproduced, stored in a retrieval system, or transmitted in any form or by any means—electronic, mechanical, photocopying, recording, or otherwise—without prior written permission of the publisher, except for brief quotations in reviews or academic citations.

This publication contains original frameworks, tools, and curriculum that are the author's intellectual property. The FLOW Execution Suite™, F.L.O.W.™, and FLOW™ are trademarked and protected content of The Chanje Collective.

Licensing and training inquiries may be directed to: dr.reba@chanjecollective.com.

First Edition

ISBN: 979-8-9992389-0-0

Cover and interior design by Dr. Reba Clarke-Wedderburn

Printed in The United States of America

Trademark Notice:

FLOW™, F.L.O.W.™, and FLOW Execution Suite™ are trademarks of The Chanje Collective. These terms refer to proprietary frameworks and tools developed by Dr. Reba Clarke-Wedderburn. They may not be copied, distributed, taught, or applied in commercial settings without explicit written permission or a licensing agreement.

To my mother,

Whose light continues to guide even in absence—the strength behind my clarity and the fire beneath my purpose.

To my three children,

Who shows me daily what it means to lead with intention, to pause with purpose, and to build with heart.

And to my father,

Who never stops evolving—proof that growth is always possible, and that leadership begins with the courage to change.

CONTENTS

Introduction	7
1. The Real Cost of Cognitive Overload	15
2. Executive Function ≠ Extra Credit	23
3. The F.L.O.W.™ Framework	35
4. Find Your Focus	43
5. Level the Task	55
6. Organize for Action	65
7. Work the Plan	75
8. Integrating F.L.O.W.™ Across Systems	87
9. Sustaining F.L.O.W.™ Over Time	97
Conclusion	109
Practical Tools & Templates for F.L.O.W.™	115
Glossary of F.L.O.W.™ Terms	143
Bibliography	145
About the Author	147

INTRODUCTION

WHY WON'T THEY JUST WORK HARDER?

Jamal sat frozen at his desk. Drowning in ten unread emails while his team meeting raged on, he felt overwhelmed—like a browser with 27 tabs open, all waiting to load but going nowhere. At 2 PM on a Tuesday, he felt lost, unsure of where to start or which words to choose.

This is just the beginning. It's a systems issue.

Leaders like Jamal confront daunting challenges daily without the essential scaffolds needed to navigate them effectively. They're expected to create clarity in conditions of chaos, build momentum inside bureaucratic fog, and coordinate action within fractured communication loops. They must respond quickly, often without the time or tools to think clearly.

Here's the truth: We're not failing because we're lazy or unfocused. We're struggling because the mental bandwidth required to function in most institutions is wildly underestimated. How we work—especially in education, nonprofits, healthcare, and other mission-driven sectors—is cognitively unsustainable.

And that strain isn't evenly distributed.

THE PROBLEM

Fast-paced workplaces often prioritize productivity at the expense of clear communication. They relentlessly pursue extra support: more meetings, emails, and tasks. But they seldom offer support for cognitive load. Result?

- Burnout disguised as busyness.
- Missed deadlines cloaked in frantic follow-ups.
- Equity gaps exist where only self-sufficient individuals can thrive.

I know this from experience. As a Black, neurodivergent professional and single mother, I intimately understand the challenges of navigating systems that favor a narrow definition of success. I witnessed brilliant educators succumb to burnout. I watched my curious, capable children being misjudged by systems that expected them to "just try harder." I felt the weight of deadlines and urgency being mistaken for effectiveness.

This isn't a motivation problem. It's a design problem.

And we can fix it.

INTRODUCTION

THE SPARK

In one meeting, where deadlines were slipping and people were running on fumes, I stopped the room and asked:

> What is our top priority this month?
> Where do we need cognitive support instead of added pressure?

That moment changed everything.

We didn't add another form, meeting, or goal. We created a **Focus Brief**: one priority, three goals, five visible tasks. Within two weeks, the fog started to clear. People felt reenergized—not because we worked harder, but because the work finally made sense.

That spark became F.L.O.W.™

INTRODUCTION

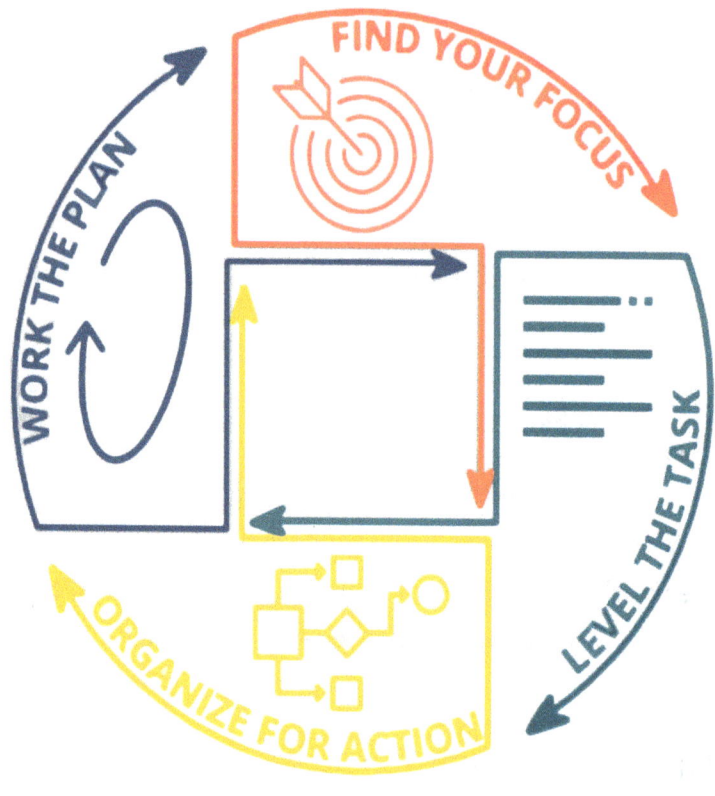

A circular diagram showing the FLOW™ cycle: Find Your Focus, Level the Task, Organize for Action, and Work the Plan in a repeating loop.

INTRODUCING F.L.O.W.™

F.L.O.W.™ is more than a checklist or mindset shift; it's a design system that drives clarity, focus, and momentum. It's built on a simple idea: cognitive scaffolding isn't optional; it's a key responsibility of leadership.

At its core are four powerful moves:

> **Find your Focus**—Clear the fog by naming priorities that ground attention and intention
> **Level the Task**—Reduce overload by breaking down complexity into manageable steps
> **Organize for Action**—Align ownership, timelines, and cognitive resources
> **Work the Plan**—Sustain execution through feedback, rhythm, and psychological safety

F.L.O.W.™ helps leaders reduce invisible cognitive load, shift from reactive to intentional, and design teams and systems where more people can thrive, not just survive.

It scales across roles and settings:

- From solo professionals to cross-functional teams
- From classrooms to cabinet-level leadership
- From nonprofits to organizational change agents

It's not just a framework. It's a commitment to clarity as a form of care.

YOUR TRANSFORMATION PROMISE

By the end of this book, you'll be ready to:

- Reclaim over 4 hours per week by reducing invisible cognitive load.

INTRODUCTION

- Reduce task churn by 30% with clear handoffs and aligned rhythms.
- Build a culture where clarity, not urgency, drives sustainable momentum.

By focusing on thoughtful design rather than simply working harder, you can transition from feeling reactive and exhausted to experiencing intentional clarity and resilient momentum.

F.L.O.W.™ is how we move from overwhelm to execution. From survival to systems. From grit to good design.

Let's get to work.

1
THE REAL COST OF COGNITIVE OVERLOAD

SCATTERED SYSTEMS DON'T JUST SLOW US DOWN—THEY BURN US OUT.

COGNITIVE OVERLOAD IS NOT a personal shortcoming; rather, it reflects a widespread structural issue that often goes unnoticed.

We've been led to believe that staying busy signifies being productive and that juggling multiple tasks at once is something to be proud of. Revised Text: Amid the constant flow of meetings, emails, and changing priorities, there is a fundamental reality we must acknowledge: we are not overwhelmed because we lack focus. Rather, we are struggling because our systems require us to manage multiple tasks and make important decisions without the support and clarity we need.

I've been there. I've witnessed how even the most talented leaders can become overwhelmed by the often-unrecognized mental burdens they carry in both education and industry. I've been in staff meetings where deadlines were missed and projects overlapped, and the usual reaction was to add more reminders and increase the pressure without taking a moment to consider:

> "What structural support is missing here?"

> The answer wasn't to try harder; it was to design better.

IT'S NOT JUST A PRODUCTIVITY PROBLEM—IT'S A JUSTICE PROBLEM

The science supports this idea. Research on executive function—our cognitive skills that help us focus, plan, adapt, and follow through—reveals that when working memory becomes overloaded, our performance can suffer, stress levels can rise, and our engagement may decrease. Acknowledging how these challenges affect our ability to function effectively is important.

> This isn't about personal grit. It's about system design.

Sweller's Cognitive Load Theory highlights an important point: when information isn't presented in a clear sequence, when tasks feel uncertain, and when priorities change unexpectedly without guidance, our brains can struggle to cope. Instead of rising to the occasion, we may feel stuck, overwhelmed, or confused (Sweller, 1988).

This impact is magnified for those navigating neurodivergence, experiencing racialized stress, and facing systemic inequity.

I've observed how neurodivergent professionals, including those with ADHD, autism, or dyslexia, often face negative labels such as "inconsistent" or "difficult" in settings that lack the external support and structure they need to thrive. I've witnessed BIPOC leaders bear the often-invisible burdens of code-switching, over-functioning, and emotional labor to keep up. This isn't about capability—it's about cognitive justice.

Cognitive Overload

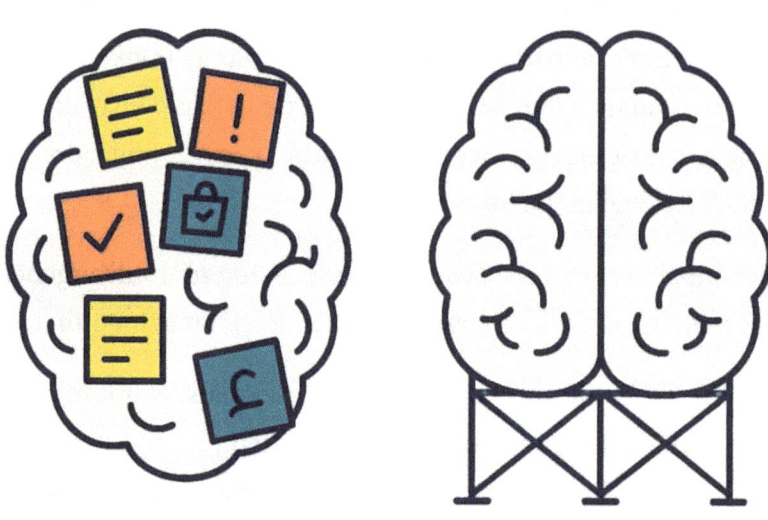

Figure: Why System Design Matters for Cognitive Load
This diagram illustrates how poorly designed systems increase invisible cognitive load, forcing individuals to rely on internal effort instead of shared scaffolding. The more the system supports clarity, the less mental energy is spent merely keeping up.

THE MASKING TRAP

Too often, high performers are praised for "resilience" or "responsiveness"—never late, always "on.". What we're truly acknowledging is the heavy toll of masking— the tiring and often unsustainable struggle to cope with the shortcomings of a flawed system.

I worked with an executive who felt overwhelmed by multiple overlapping projects. When we introduced a weekly Task Clarity Brief, her first reaction was: "I thought this was just for people with ADHD." Two weeks later, her clarity and energy returned. She wasn't fixing a personal flaw but shedding an unfair burden.

This is the frequently overlooked impact of cognitive overload:

- Energy lost to ambiguity.
- Talent is wasted in reactive cycles.
- Equity is undermined by systems that favor those who can self-scaffold.

We lose brilliance—not because people are unmotivated, but because they're overtaxed and under-supported.

That's why supporting executive function isn't just helpful—it's a leadership responsibility.

A LEADERSHIP RESPONSIBILITY

Supporting executive function isn't an accommodation; it's a design imperative. When leaders establish clear priorities, organize tasks logically, identify key starting points, and incorporate feedback mechanisms, they are not simply protecting their team but fostering an environment that promotes sustainable performance and fairness for everyone.

That's the work of The F.L.O.W.™ Coaching Framework.

- **Find your Focus** to name what matters and initiate momentum.

- **Level the Task** to cut through ambiguity and define next steps.
- **Organize for Action** to sequence work into manageable parts.
- **Work the Plan** to sustain progress with built-in feedback and support.

This isn't just another management fad or checklist. It's a system designed to externalize clarity, reduce friction, and build resilience—because clarity isn't a perk—it's a leadership responsibility.

≈ PAUSE. SPARK. ACT

Where in your team's workflows are people carrying invisible cognitive load?

How might clearer scaffolding—not more reminders—ease the strain?

What's one change you could implement this week that would help clarify things and encourage meaningful progress?

THE COST OF DOING NOTHING

If we don't design for clarity, we will continue to lose brilliant people to burnout, disengagement, or quiet compliance. We continue to encourage over-functioning and masking behaviors, often failing to recognize the significant toll that cognitive overload takes on individuals.

THE REAL COST OF COGNITIVE OVERLOAD

This isn't about seeking acts of heroism. It's a call for systems that work **with** the brain, not against it.

In the next chapter, we'll explore why executive function isn't a bonus skill; it's the cognitive backbone of sustainable leadership.

2
EXECUTIVE FUNCTION ≠ EXTRA CREDIT

RETHINKING EF AS A BASELINE REQUIREMENT, NOT A BONUS SKILL

AT 11:00 AM, Jordan stared at his third unread email about a delayed report. Although his calendar appeared clear, his mind was overwhelmed—tasks were vying for his attention, each feeling just as urgent as the last. He wasn't ignoring the work. He had no ramp to begin with.

That's the invisible weight of executive function (EF) breakdown. And it's not a personal shortcoming; it's a design flaw.

WHAT IS EXECUTIVE FUNCTION?

Executive function refers to a set of cognitive processes essential for goal-directed behavior, including planning, working memory, attention, problem-solving, verbal reasoning, inhibition, mental flexibility, task switching, and initiating and monitoring actions. These functions are primarily associated with the prefrontal cortex of the brain.

When our executive function is overwhelmed by chaotic workflows, constantly changing priorities, or a lack of supportive structures, it becomes difficult for us to focus and stay engaged. The mind can feel overwhelmed and stuck; sometimes, our strongest determination isn't enough to move us forward.

Figure: What Cognitive Overload Looks Like *When systems don't scaffold clarity, there is a cost. It's not just a busy calendar; it's a mind juggling deadlines, priorities, and unspoken expectations, all while trying to look like it's under control.*

This is where most systems fail. They assume EF is infinite and everyone can either "focus more" or "stay organized." But that's not how brains work, especially under pressure.

THE MYTH OF EF AS A BONUS SKILL

Too often, organizations treat executive function as if it were an extra credit assignment. If you can juggle multiple projects, adapt on the fly, and prioritize yourself amidst chaos, you're seen as a high performer. If you can't, you are labeled as inconsistent or underperforming.

This isn't just about what each person can do on their own. It's about systemic scaffolding.

Those who appear to "just get it" often draw strength from unseen resources, such as privileged access to informal networks, unspoken cultural norms, or personal coping strategies developed over time. Without those, even the most capable brains can hit cognitive overload.

EF doesn't feel optional until it fails.

> X Missed deadlines? ☞ Blame the person.
> X Incomplete projects? ☞ Blame the person.
> X Lack of follow-through? ☞ Blame the person.

> But the real issue isn't the person. It's the system.

THE HIDDEN COST OF MASKING

I coached a leader who was praised for her responsiveness—always available and on top of things. Deep down, she felt utterly exhausted. She filled clarity gaps daily, drafted last-minute agendas, and rescued stalled projects.

When we rolled out the weekly Task Clarity Brief, she was skeptical. "Isn't this just for people who struggle with focus?"

TASK CLARITY BRIEF

Task:	Redesign PD deck for equity strand
Entry Point:	Open template, re-sequence 4 slides based on the new outline
Example Steps:	• Review Jasmine's feedback • Revise Slide Order • Add 2 content slides • Upload to library
Docs:	last year's deck DEI outline PDF
Owner:	Alex R.
Next:	Friday, the next sprint meeting

Figure: What Task Clarity Looks Like in Practice *"Redesign the PD deck" isn't a task—it's a project hiding inside a sentence.*

Two weeks later, she wasn't just more organized; she was less drained. The scaffolding didn't just address a weakness; it provided support to help alleviate an unseen burden within the system.

F.L.O.W.™ THE EQUITY-CENTERED COACHING FRAMEWORK

Figure: The 9 Executive Function Skills *These nine interconnected abilities help us plan, focus, regulate, and follow through.*

> Executive function isn't one skill—it's a system.

When we design environments that support them, we reduce friction, not just for a few, but for everyone.

SYSTEMIC EQUITY STARTS WITH COGNITIVE DESIGN

Unstructured environments can significantly hinder progress and have a detrimental impact on individuals. They reward those with unspoken privileges and leave everyone else scrambling.

The cost is even higher for neurodivergent professionals, caregivers, and BIPOC leaders. They're expected to perform at high capacity without the cognitive scaffolding that makes this possible. Over time, this leads to chronic stress, reduced confidence, and disengagement.

Here's the shift we need:

- Scaffolding isn't hand-holding; it's leadership design.
- EF isn't extra; it's the backbone of sustainable, equitable systems.

F.L.O.W.™ THE EQUITY-CENTERED COACHING FRAMEWORK

Figure: Same wall. Different tools. One person climbs with support. The other has to balance, reach, and hope the ladder holds. That's the difference system design makes. Executive function isn't about trying harder—it's about having scaffolding that actually works.

THE RESEARCH BEHIND THE SHIFT

Working memory has a limited capacity, and instructional design should aim to reduce unnecessary cognitive load to optimize learning (Sweller, 1988). Minimizing extraneous load and enhancing meaningful (germane) load facilitate better processing and retention.

Baddeley's model of working memory emphasizes that the central executive, which is responsible for directing our attention and managing our thought processes, can sometimes feel overwhelmed. This overload can make it more challenging to stay focused and engage in purposeful actions (Baddeley & Hitch, 1974).

The central executive plays a crucial role in coordinating different systems, such as the phonological loop and visuospatial sketchpad, which work together to help us tackle complex cognitive tasks like reasoning and understanding.

Individuals who experience challenges with executive functioning often face decreased work engagement and diminished employee well-being. Their findings suggest enhancing executive function can improve job satisfaction and overall mental health.

This is not simply about encouraging people to work harder. It's about establishing systems that reduce mental strain so that clarity becomes the norm rather than a rare occurrence.

≈ PAUSE. SPARK. ACT

> Where are we relying on individuals to fill in the gaps caused by a lack of structure?

> How could a single change in our system help support better focus, planning, and follow-through for everyone involved?

> Who on your team might be masking cognitive strain, and how can you make it visible and provide support?

THE PATH FORWARD

Understanding that effective frameworks are vital, infrastructure shifts leadership from simply responding to challenges to actively designing solutions. Our goal is to minimize confusion, establish supportive structures, and develop systems that ensure everyone has an equal opportunity to achieve clarity and make a meaningful impact, regardless of how their brains work.

In the next chapter, we'll delve into the F.L.O.W.™ framework, a thoughtful approach that provides clarity and support without placing the burden of resilience on individuals.

3
THE F.L.O.W.™ FRAMEWORK

DESIGNING FOR COGNITIVE CLARITY, SUSTAINED FOCUS, AND EQUITY

FOR YEARS, I watched brilliant, driven leaders struggle to maintain clarity and momentum in the face of relentless complexity. I could relate to their experience—always responding to new challenges, moving quickly from one task to another, and feeling the heavy burden of uncertainty and the pressure to succeed. I didn't realize that the system wasn't aligned with how our brains naturally function.

This book was created to address that gap.

The F.L.O.W.™ framework was born not only from research but also from necessity. This idea arose from the intersection of cognitive science, real-world leadership experiences, and a profound recognition of the vital connections between equity, clarity, and engagement. F.L.O.W.™ is not just a concept; it's a practice. This dynamic framework is designed to support leaders in organizing their thoughts, maintaining focus, and fostering environments where clarity and equity are not merely goals but everyday practices.

THE SCIENCE BEHIND THE FRAMEWORK

Cognitive science tells us that our brains are not built for unstructured chaos. Cognitive Load Theory (Sweller, 1988) emphasizes that our working memory, which has limited capacity, can easily become overwhelmed when we encounter unclear, complex, or contradictory information. This can make processing and understanding challenging for many individuals. When this happens, decision-making falters, attention fractures, and engagement erodes.

In leadership, this looks like endless meetings with no clear outcomes, shifting priorities without a structured response, and relying on individuals to "figure it out" under pressure. It's not a people problem; it's a design problem.

Research on executive function (EF)—which includes important cognitive processes like planning, attention, working memory, and self-regulation (Diamond, 2013; Barkley, 2012)—shows that the ability to maintain clarity and adaptability is not an innate trait, but rather skills that can be developed over time. These abilities are nurtured and developed, significantly shaped by the surrounding environment and the support systems.

When organizations do not offer external support systems,

individuals are challenged to manage everything on their own. This situation particularly affects neurodivergent leaders, BIPOC professionals, and individuals facing systemic inequities, making it necessary for them to hide their cognitive overload, overexert themselves, and ultimately experience burnout.

F.L.O.W.™ DISRUPTS THIS CYCLE.

F.L.O.W.™ transforms confusion and uncertainty into purposeful, thoughtful design. It offers a scaffold aligned with how the brain processes complexity and how equity demands clarity.

THE ANATOMY OF F.L.O.W.™

At its essence, F.L.O.W.™ represents an ongoing journey rather than a simple linear checklist. It is thoughtfully designed to adjust to changing situations, ensuring communication remains clear, engaging, and impactful. Each phase addresses a distinct aspect of executive function.

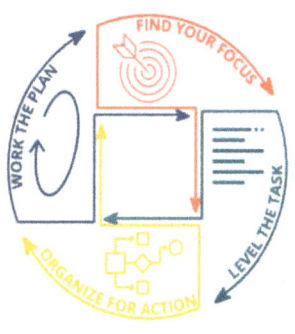

Figure: The F.L.O.W.™ Framework

1. FIND YOUR FOCUS

This phase clears the fog. Research indicates that identifying a specific goal or priority can significantly reduce cognitive load and enhance the efficiency of our working memory (Gollwitzer, 1999).

In practice, this means pausing to ask:

> What matters most right now?
>
> What is the single, non-negotiable priority?

By anchoring our focus, we create cognitive space to engage meaningfully.

2. Level the Task

This phase breaks complexity into sequenced, manageable actions. Cognitive Load Theory and studies on chunking (Miller, 1956) show that our brains process information better when broken into smaller, coherent units. This step also promotes fairness, ensuring everyone can access clear information, regardless of their background or insider knowledge.

3. Organize for Action

With focus and clearly defined tasks, we now move to execution. This phase draws on metacognition research (Zimmerman, 2002), emphasizing planning, sequencing, and feedback. Leaders align responsibilities, set timelines, and create external structures—replacing mental juggling with visible, shared clarity.

4. Work the Plan

Sustained momentum requires rhythm and adaptability. This phase integrates flow theory (Csikszentmihalyi, 1990) and research on psychological safety (Edmondson, 1999). It offers regular check-ins, opportunities for reflection, and chances to discuss any obstacles you may face. When teams feel secure in adjusting, their ability to execute becomes flexible and strong rather than fragile.

WHY F.L.O.W.™ IS DIFFERENT

While traditional coaching models such as Knight's Impact Cycle, Cognitive Coaching, and GROW emphasize individual autonomy and goal-setting, F.L.O.W.™ takes a more holistic approach by incorporating executive function science, flow theory, and a strong commitment to equity.

It acknowledges that clarity is essential for productivity and a vital matter of fairness and justice. When systems rely on chance for clarity, they tend to favor those who already have built-in support or advantages. F.L.O.W.™ democratizes clarity by making it a design feature rather than an individual responsibility.

F.L.O.W.™ THE EQUITY-CENTERED COACHING FRAMEWORK

Comprehensive Comparative Matrix of Coaching Models

Feature	F.L.O.W.™	GROW	CLEAR	Co-Active	Instructional Coaching
Structured Cognitive Support	Strong	Moderate	Moderate	Weak	Moderate
Executive Function Integration	Strong	Weak	Weak	Weak	Moderate
Equity Focused and Inclusive Approach	Strong	Weak	Moderate	Moderate	Moderate
Robust Tools for High Pressure Environments	Strong	Moderate	Moderate	Weak	Moderate
Data Driven Continuous Feedback Loops	Strong	Moderate	Moderate	Weak	Strong

✓ Strong | ❗ Moderate | ✗ Weak

Figure: Why F.L.O.W.™ Stands Out

Compared to GROW, CLEAR, Co-Active, and Instructional Coaching, F.L.O.W.™:

- Clarity is supported by external resources rather than relying solely on individual effort.
- Tasks are designed to promote long-term cognitive well-being rather than simply maximizing output.
- Engagement is designed into the system, building resilience
- Equity is operationalized, ensuring clarity for all brains in all contexts

This unique combination makes F.L.O.W.™ a leader in modern coaching and organizational performance.

A LIVING SYSTEM

F.L.O.W.™ is not static.

It adapts to the demands of our work environment and leadership challenges, making it valuable in coaching conversations, during team projects, or in driving organizational initiatives. Its strength comes from its ability to adapt: the loop can tighten or expand depending on the situation, yet the core principles remain the same.

This chapter lays the foundation. In the next sections, we'll detail each phase of F.L.O.W.™ in detail, providing real-world examples, reflection tools, and actionable templates to embed this framework into your leadership practice.

> Clarity is not a luxury—it's a right.

4
FIND YOUR FOCUS

THE SCIENCE AND PRACTICE OF CLARITY

JAMAL'S CALENDAR burst with back-to-back meetings, follow-up emails, and a flood of competing requests. By midday, he was juggling so many responsibilities that each felt equally urgent and important. Yet nothing was progressing.

This was not a time management problem. The breakdown in focus stemmed from cognitive overload and a lack of external clarity.

In leadership, clarity means not just deciding what to focus on but also strategically narrowing attention, easing cognitive strain, and fostering sustained engagement. Start the F.L.O.W.™ cycle: **Zero in on Your Focus.**

Figure: Clarity starts with choosing one thing. *When everything feels urgent, it's easy to get pulled in a dozen directions.*

THE COGNITIVE SCIENCE OF FOCUS

OUR BRAINS ARE DESIGNED to prioritize survival over strategy. The prefrontal cortex—responsible for executive functions like working memory and focus—can manage only a limited number of complex tasks at once (Diamond, 2013;

Barkley, 2012). When cognitive load becomes excessive—due to ambiguous tasks, shifting goals, or emotional stress—our attention becomes fragmented.

Research on cognitive load theory (Sweller, 1988) confirms that working memory capacity is sharply limited. When overloaded, performance declines, decision-making suffers, and the brain shifts from a proactive to a reactive state.

In fast-paced leadership environments, leaders can't just "try harder" to concentrate. They need external structures to alleviate cognitive strain.

Additionally, Gollwitzer's (1999) research on implementation intentions shows that when we explicitly connect context—the "when" and "where"—with action—the "what"—we significantly increase the likelihood of follow-through. This insight underpins the **Find Your Focus** phase: by identifying what matters most in the current context, leaders anchor attention and create cognitive traction.

Figure: The Iceberg of Visible Work *Meetings, emails, and deliverables reveal only the surface; beneath lies the hidden cognitive labor—deciphering vague expectations, adapting to shifting goals, and supporting oneself under pressure—that many leaders bear in silence.*

WHY FOCUS IS A JUSTICE ISSUE

> Clarity isn't a luxury—it's an equity imperative.

In systems where the loudest voices or most privileged perspectives dominate, ambiguity often conceals inequities. Neurodivergent leaders, BIPOC professionals, and those navigating complex cultural landscapes usually bear the burden of invisible cognitive labor: interpreting unclear expectations, managing shifting goals, and self-scaffolding under pressure.

Find Your Focus is not about enforcing a rigid priority list. It's about disrupting those inequities by making clarity visible, shared, and actionable. When priorities are transparent, everyone has equal access to direction and decision-making power.

THE PRACTICE OF FOCUS

Finding your focus is not a one-time decision; it's a disciplined practice of returning to clarity amid complexity. Here's how to do it:

1. NAME THE PRIORITY

Identify the single most critical priority for the current timeframe. Research suggests that explicitly naming a goal reduces cognitive noise and sharpens attention (Gollwitzer, 1999).

> Instead of: "Stay on top of budget items."

> Try: "This week, our priority is finalizing the Q3 budget proposal."

2. Sequence the Steps

Break the priority into no more than 3 to 5 actionable goals or milestones. This leverages the brain's natural capacity for chunking (Miller, 1956), reducing the chance of cognitive overload.

3. Contextualize the Focus

Tie the priority to a specific timeframe or event.

> Example: "We will finalize the Q3 budget proposal during Wednesday's strategy meeting."

This approach harnesses implementation intentions to enhance follow-through.

4. Make It Visible

Display the priority and subgoals where your team can see them: in a shared workspace, on a task board, or in a digital collaboration tool. Visibility reduces reliance on memory and ensures collective alignment.

5. ALIGN THE LANGUAGE

Use clear and direct phrasing. Avoid jargon and vague language.

> Better: "Finalize budget proposal by Friday."

> Avoid: "Wrap up budget discussion."

HARD-WON LESSON: THE FOCUS BRIEF

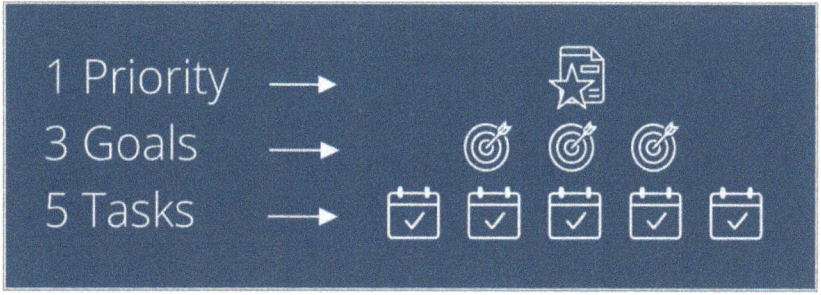

Clarity in Practice – This is an overview of the Focus Brief structure.

At an educational nonprofit, the leadership team was overwhelmed by conflicting initiatives. When we introduced a simple Focus Brief—a one-page summary of the week's priorities, subgoals, and key deadlines—the effect was immediate. Meetings became more focused.

Task ownership became clearer. Cognitive load was visibly lightened.

One leader remarked, 'For the first time, I don't feel like I'm trying to read minds.' We're all aligned on what matters."

This was a shift in system design, not just in work ethic.

≈ PAUSE. SPARK. ACT

> What competing priorities are fragmenting your focus right now?
>
> > What's your top non-negotiable priority for this week?
>
> How can you make that focus clear and actionable for your team?
>
> > Who on your team might benefit the most from shared clarity?

THE POWER OF FOCUS

Focus is not about narrowing ambition; it's about creating cognitive breathing room so that complex, meaningful work can take root. When leaders make focus explicit and shared, they not only drive productivity—they build resilience, foster equity, and create momentum.

In the next chapter, we will explore the second quadrant of F.L.O.W.™: **Level the Task**—where we move from clarity to structure, breaking down complex work into manageable, sequenced actions that reduce overload and sustain execution.

Because clarity isn't an individual virtue; it's a collective design principle.

F.L.O.W.™ THE EQUITY-CENTERED COACHING FRAMEWORK

EF-WC-001: Focus Brief

F.L.O.W.™ Quadrant: F – Find Your Focus
EF Skills Supported: Planning, Attention, Self-Monitoring
Best-Matched Strategy: Goal Chunking, Visual Anchoring
Format: Fillable Brief + Team-Facing Usage Guide

Purpose	To reduce overwhelm and sharpen task alignment by clearly defining the one top priority, aligned goals, and visible actions.
When to Use This Tool	<ul><li>Weekly team planning or kickoff</li><li>New project or sprint launch</li><li>When priorities feel scattered or reactive</li></ul>
Step-by-Step Instructions	1. **Name the Priority** One main objective. Use a behavior-focused action (e.g., "Draft onboarding guide"). 2. **Set 3 Meaningful Goals** ○ Milestone-style goals are aligned with the priority. ○ Use verbs like deliver, finalize, and align. 3. **List 5 Visible Tasks** ○ Concrete steps you can see or check off. ○ Avoid vague actions like "think about..." 4. **Check for Cognitive Fit** Ask: Is this visible? Reasonable? Sequenced? 5. **Anchor in Rhythm** ○ Share in the team space ○ Refer to it in weekly standups or 1:1s
Template	→ **This Week's Priority:** [One behavioral objective] → **3 Supporting Goals:** → **5 Visible Tasks:** → **Owner:** → **Check-in Point:**
Coaching Tip	Ask: "What's your one thing right now? What would be enough to say it's moving?"

FLOW Execution Suite™ and its tools are part of the protected FLOW™ Executive Function System.
©2025. All rights reserved. For licensed use only.
Structure clarity. Support focus. Scale momentum.

Figure: Focus Brief – A tool for clarifying priorities and anchoring clarity at the start of each week or project. The Focus Brief transforms reactive work into purposeful action. Leaders reduce overwhelm by setting one priority, three aligned goals, and five visible tasks, and establishing a clear vision for the week.

"Clarity isn't about doing more—it's about doing what matters."

5
LEVEL THE TASK

BREAKING COMPLEXITY INTO COGNITIVE CLARITY

THE LEADERSHIP TEAM gathered around the conference table, glancing nervously at a project plan that sprawled across four pages. Everyone agreed that the initiative was important, but no one knew where to begin. The scope was so vast and tangled that it felt easier to discuss deadlines than to design a clear path forward.

This isn't a rare scenario. It's the predictable outcome of unstructured complexity—a system that demands cognitive effort without providing the scaffolding to manage it.

Level the Task, the second quadrant of the F.L.O.W.™ framework, directly addresses this. It's the design response to what cognitive science tells us about how the human brain handles complexity, ambiguity, and overload.

Figure: The Priority Compass *When everything feels important, this tool helps leaders stay grounded. The five anchors—People, Purpose, Progress, Pause, and Driver—clarify what matters most in the moment, ensuring that action is guided by intention, not urgency.*

THE SCIENCE OF TASK STRUCTURING

Our brains are not wired for endless multitasking or for holding complex, unstructured information in working memory. Cognitive Load Theory (Sweller, 1988) demonstrates that when the intrinsic load of a task (its natural complexity) is combined with extraneous load (such as confusing instructions and unclear goals), working memory can become overwhelmed. This doesn't just slow us down—it leads to cognitive fatigue, decision paralysis, and disengagement.

Research on chunking (Miller, 1956) shows that breaking information into manageable units enables our brains to process, retain, and act on it more effectively. This principle isn't just for memory; it's crucial for leadership.

Task structuring is a vital equity practice. For leaders from marginalized communities, such as BIPOC and neurodivergent professionals, unstructured complexity, micro and macro norms often heighten barriers. Those lacking informal networks or cultural norms must shoulder the burden of "figuring it out" alone.

Clear, leveled tasks enhance cognitive flow and democratize clarity.

THE FOUR ELEMENTS OF LEVELING THE TASK

1. Deconstruct the Complexity

Begin by pinpointing the main task or goal. Divide it into 3 to 5 distinct components or phases, each serving a clear purpose.

For instance, "Launch a new client onboarding system" transforms into:

- Draft initial workflows
- Review legal compliance
- Pilot with select clients
- Refine based on feedback

- Full implementation

This step aligns with metacognitive research (Zimmerman, 2002), demonstrating that explicit planning boosts engagement and persistence.

Figure: The Gap Between What's Said and What's Understood *"Design the newsletter" seems straightforward—until you face the ambiguity yourself. This image showcases the transition from vague instructions to clear, structured tasks. It's not about ability; it's about clarity.*

2. Clarify Entry Points

Clearly define the starting point. Cognitive psychology (Gollwitzer, 1999) reveals that many tasks falter at the starting line.

Instead of: "Revamp marketing materials,"

Try: "Monday: Draft homepage copy."

3. Sequence for Momentum

Organize tasks strategically to generate cognitive momentum. Research on cognitive flexibility (Diamond, 2013) reveals that the brain thrives on structured and meaningful sequences. Start with clear, actionable steps to inspire a sense of progress.

4. Visualize the Flow

Leverage task boards, timelines, and flowcharts to visualize your work. Enhanced visibility reduces cognitive load and fosters a unified understanding within the team.

> In one instance, a school leadership team implemented a color-coded task board to clarify the prep, review, and implementation stages—slashing confusion and reducing rework cycles by 40%.

HARD-WON LESSON: MAYA'S PROJECT RESCUE

Maya, a program manager at a community health organization, was assigned to launch a new mental health initiative. The scope was immense: engaging stakeholders, allocating resources, training staff, and overhauling data systems. Meetings turned into frantic firefighting.

Using **Level the Task,** Maya empowered her team to:

- Break the initiative into four clear phases
- Identify starting tasks for each phase
- Create a shared visual timeline with color-coded priorities
- Assign task ownership with weekly check-ins

Within a month, the overwhelming was transformed into actionable steps. Staff felt empowered, never overwhelmed. Maya noted, it wasn't a lack of skills—it was the overwhelming scope of the work that blurred our vision. Breaking down the task made it achievable.

≈ PAUSE. SPARK. ACT

Where is complexity hindering momentum in your project or team?

How can you simplify the work into fewer, clearer phases or tasks?

What's one task you can tackle right now?

Who could benefit from a visual task map to eliminate ambiguity?

WHY LEVELING MATTERS

Level the Task transcends project planning. It transforms overwhelm into clarity and ambiguity into action. It's about equity—making clarity a shared resource for everyone, not just the experienced or well connected, to support widespread success.

In the next chapter, we shift from a clear understanding to coordinated action with **Organize for Action,** focusing on building ownership, establishing timelines, and implementing feedback systems that drive momentum and resilience.

> Clarity isn't the goal; it's the foundation.

F.L.O.W.™ THE EQUITY-CENTERED COACHING FRAMEWORK

EF-WC-003: Task Clarity Brief

F.L.O.W.™ Quadrant: L – Level the Task
EF Skills Supported: Task Initiation, Planning, Working Memory
Best-Matched Strategy: Behavioral Activation, Sequencing, Externalization
Format: Fillable Brief + Team-Facing Usage Guide

Purpose	Break down vague or cognitively heavy tasks into clear, startable steps. It prevents stalling, fog, and ambiguity.
When to Use This Tool	• Before assigning cognitively heavy tasks • When someone delays starting • During kickoff or sprint planning • When mental fog is high

Step-by-Step Instructions	1. **Write the Task in Behavioral Language**
	e.g., "Draft curriculum flow options," not "Figure out the curriculum."
	2. **Define What 'Start' Looks Like**
	Ask: "What would I see you doing if you started?"
	3. **Break the Task into 3-5 Steps**
	  ◦ Visible, sequenced, and grounded in action.
	4. **Add Scaffolds**
	Share examples, templates, or visuals that guide the work.
	5. **Confirm Ownership and Check-In**
	  ◦ Clarify who owns it and when it will be revisited.

Template	→ Task: [Behavioral description] → What counts as "starting"? [Describe first action] → Steps to Complete: → Links, Docs, or Examples Provided: [Paste or attach] → Owner: → Next Check-In:
Coaching Tip	"What would count as starting?" Use this when a task feels mentally stuck or delayed.

FLOW Execution Suite™ and its tools are part of the protected FLOW™ Executive Function System.
©2025. All rights reserved. For licensed use only.
Structure clarity. Support focus. Scale momentum.

Figure: Task Clarity Brief – Simplifying complex tasks into actionable steps. One person hears, "Design the newsletter", and freezes. The other feature is a Task Clarity Brief—actionable steps, a clear starting point, and driving momentum. Leveling the task means cutting through ambiguity to initiate the work.

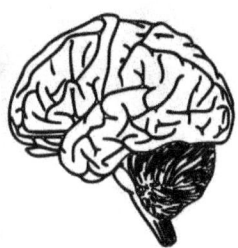

"Neurodiverse leadership isn't a challenge—it's an untapped source of clarity and momentum."

6
ORGANIZE FOR ACTION

MOVING FROM CLARITY TO EXECUTION WITH PURPOSEFUL DESIGN

AFTER TWO WEEKS of intense effort, Maya's team transformed their complex initiative into tiered tasks with a clear visual timeline. Yet progress began to falter once more. Meetings meandered, ownership faded, and follow-through faltered.

Many well-intentioned initiatives falter not due to unclear goals, but because of poor execution. Clarity without organization is like a map without a compass: it points the way but doesn't drive you forward.

Organize for Action, the third quadrant of the F.L.O.W.™ framework, fills this gap by transforming clarity into coordinated momentum, embedding structures that align ownership, timelines, and feedback with how our brains and teams function.

Figure: Turning Deadlines into Anchors for Clarity *The task list is just one piece of the puzzle. This team visualizes work on a calendar, aligning roles, timelines, and steps to maintain momentum amidst the weekly shuffle. Sequencing isn't just planning; it's the backbone of follow-through.*

THE SCIENCE OF COORDINATED ACTION

Cognitive science and behavioral research show that sustained action relies not only on willpower but also on design.

Implementation Intention Theory (Gollwitzer, 1999) shows that linking intentions to specific contexts (e.g., "When X happens, I will do Y") dramatically boosts follow-through. Abstract goals like "Work on budget proposal", gain traction when transformed into time-bound, context-specific commitments like "At 10 AM Monday, draft the budget summary."

Metacognitive research (Zimmerman, 2002) demonstrates that structured planning and continuous self-monitoring boost persistence and adaptability.

Leaders ease cognitive strain and pave the way for action by establishing external structures such as timelines, role clarity, and progress checkpoints.

Psychological safety (Edmondson, 1999) highlights that when people feel safe voicing blockers or modifying plans, teams build greater resilience and adaptability. Without safety, ambiguity festers, and feedback loops break down.

ROLE MAPPING EXAMPLE

Initiative: Summer 2025 PD Series

AREA	DRIVER	SUPPORT	RHYTHM	LINK
Slides	Taylor H.	Jordan (content)	Weekly 1:1	Notion > slide decks
Registration	Diego M.	Tania (data)	As needed	Google Sheet Tracker
Facilitation	Jae Y.	Team Leads	Bi-weekly Huddle	PD Launch Plan Doc

Review Rhythm: Monthly team planning
Notes: Jordan will step into the lead role next cycle

Figure: Role Mapping Makes Ownership Visible *Vague ownership leads to stalled accountability. This map identifies who is driving, who is supporting, and when they connect—ensuring clarity on roles and timelines.*

THE THREE PILLARS OF ORGANIZING FOR ACTION

1. Align Ownership

Why it matters: Unclear ownership causes tasks to drift, wasting energy on determining responsibility, which leads to delays and missed deadlines.

How to apply: Assign a single owner for each task or deliverable, even in collaborative work. Use shared documentation (such as a task tracker or charter) to visualize this ownership.

> Example: A project charter that assigns milestone owners sharpens accountability and reduces ambiguity.

2. Set Timelines and Context

Why it matters: Vague timelines create either false urgency or endless delays. The brain needs anchored targets to initiate and maintain action.

How to apply: Replace general deadlines with specific contextual checkpoints.

> Instead of: "Finish report by Friday."

> Use: "By Friday at 2 PM, submit the executive summary draft for peer review."

This small shift eliminates decision fatigue and strengthens accountability.

3. Embed Feedback Loops

Why it matters: Progress stalls when there is no feedback. Teams either forge ahead blindly or hesitate because of uncertainty. Structured check-ins reduce friction and increase resilience.

How to apply: Introduce rhythm-based check-ins—daily stand-ups, weekly huddles, and mid-point reviews—where blockers can be surfaced, course corrections can be made, and wins can be celebrated.

> Example: A school leadership team implemented biweekly "clarity huddles," which cut decision backlogs by half and made support needs visible in real time.

F.L.O.W.™ THE EQUITY-CENTERED COACHING FRAMEWORK

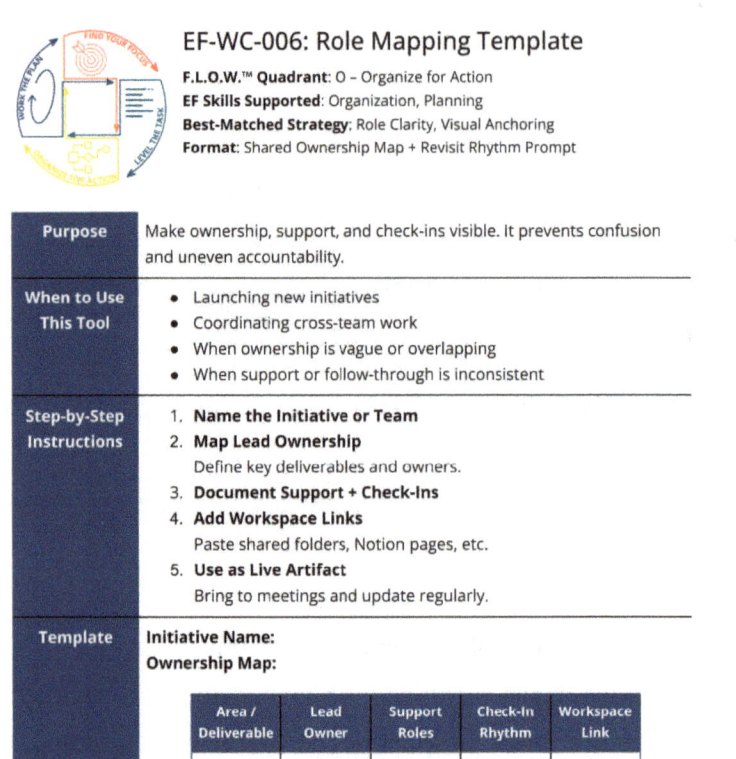

Figure: Role Mapping – Define shared ownership and clarify roles. This tool clarifies who is driving, who is supporting, and how they will stay aligned. It's not just about task assignment—it's about establishing lasting clarity across weeks, roles, and rhythms.

HARD-WON LESSON: NIA'S DISTRIBUTED OWNERSHIP

Nia, a district education leader, was charged with launching a multi-school reading intervention. Her initial plan depended on district staff to facilitate the rollout. Progress was uneven, and expectations remained vague.

Using **Organize for Action**, Nia:

- Created a clear ownership matrix, assigning deliverables to school-based teams with one named contact per task
- Connected deadlines to existing events for context (e.g., "Submit reading data by October PD day").
- Introduced biweekly feedback huddles where teams shared updates, identified blockers, and reallocated resources

In just one quarter, the initiative's completion rate surged by 60%. Teams experienced greater clarity, reduced stress, and increased engagement. Nia reflected, we didn't just gain clarity—we deepened our connection. Everyone knew their role and felt empowered to execute it.

≈ PAUSE. SPARK. ACT

> Where is ownership unclear or fragmented in your current projects?

> How can you replace vague deadlines with clear, contextual checkpoints?

> Which straightforward feedback loop can enhance adaptability and simplify decision making?
>
> > Which team members need explicit support to identify blockers or request adjustments?

THE EQUITY IMPERATIVE

Organizing for action goes beyond efficiency; it's about fairness. In poorly structured systems, those with systemic advantages—such as network access and knowledge of unspoken norms—navigate ambiguity with greater ease. Neurodivergent and BIPOC leaders shoulder the invisible burden of navigating the system.

Organize for Action ensures equitable clarity and support by explicitly sharing ownership, timelines, and feedback. It alleviates self-scaffolding and fosters an environment in which everyone can thrive.

LOOKING AHEAD

In the next chapter, we finalize the F.L.O.W.™ loop with **Work the Plan**—unpacking how to embed execution rhythms, flexibility, and psychological safety to maintain momentum and achieve lasting progress. Clarity isn't enough; it must be acted on.

"Priorities don't need to be perfect. They need to be clear, actionable, and aligned with values."

7
WORK THE PLAN

EMBEDDING RHYTHMS FOR SUSTAINABLE EXECUTION AND ADAPTABILITY

NIA'S DISTRICT-WIDE reading initiative was in full swing. Ownership was defined, timelines were set, and feedback loops were established. But three weeks in, the familiar pattern returned: clarity was slipping away. Updates lagged. Teams stalled in addressing the blockers. Urgent tasks began to overshadow important ones.

Well-structured plans often lose momentum in this way. It's not due to carelessness or disengagement. Systems that fail to embed execution into rhythm inevitably become reactive.

Work the Plan, the final quadrant of the F.L.O.W.™ framework, tackles this challenge head-on. Design execution that thrives without individual heroics or micromanagement. It fosters sustainable momentum through built-in rhythms, psychological safety, and adaptability, grounded in cognitive science and real-world experience.

Figure: Visibility Builds Shared Momentum *This team uses a shared task board to track progress and eliminate ambiguity—no guessing involved. Execution accelerates when everyone can see what's next and what has been completed.*

THE SCIENCE OF SUSTAINABLE EXECUTION

Neuroscience and organizational research reveal why plans stall.

Cognitive Load Theory (Sweller, 1988) highlights that when our working memory becomes overwhelmed—due to shifting priorities, unclear next steps, or insufficient feedback—our ability to execute tasks can suffer. Cognitive energy is often consumed not only by completing tasks but also by the effort of anticipating what needs to be done next.

Flow Theory, as outlined by Csikszentmihalyi in 1990, highlights how we experience a sense of fulfillment and achieve our best work when we have clear goals, receive immediate feedback, and engage in tasks that match our skill levels.

Psychological safety (Edmondson, 1999) shows that teams thrive when it is safe to surface problems, admit uncertainty, and request help. In its absence, blockers remain hidden, bottlenecks grow, and momentum dissolves.

Adaptive Leadership (Heifetz & Linsky, 2002) emphasizes that when faced with complex challenges, it is essential to have systems that can adjust their actions while still maintaining a clear sense of purpose.

> Structure sustains energy. Safety sustains adaptability. Rhythm sustains momentum.

F.L.O.W.™ THE EQUITY-CENTERED COACHING FRAMEWORK

Sample Rhythm Map

FLOW CYCLE: Q3 Assessment Sprint

Checkpoint	Owner	Timing	Format	Notes/Link
Kickoff	Jordan R.	Monday 10am	Zoom	Slides in Notion
Prioritization Briefs	Leads	Monday PM	Notion	Focus Briefs link
Feedback	Program	Friday	Async	
Weekly Sync	Team	Wed 2pm	Zoom	Notes / Docs
Handoff Review	Ops	Friday 3pm	Slack	Checklist
Retro & Reflect	Facilitator	Last Friday	Live	Update Rhythm Map

Figure: Rhythm Maps Make Momentum Visible *This rhythm map translates abstract routines into a concrete system. It outlines when each checkpoint occurs, who owns it, and how it's shared—so clarity isn't left to memory or luck.*

THE THREE ANCHORS OF WORKING THE PLAN

1. Establish Execution Rhythms

Why it matters: Without rhythm, plans stall. Predictable routines reduce cognitive load and help maintain focus.

How to apply: Build regular cycles—daily stand-ups, weekly sprints, and monthly reviews—that match the complexity and pace of your work.

Example: A nonprofit team added 15-minute daily

check-ins. Within a quarter, task completion rose by 40%.

These short, predictable routines create accountability without micromanagement.

2. Create Safe Feedback Channels

Why it matters: Execution falters when problems are hidden. Teams need safe spaces to surface blockers early and adjust their course quickly.

How to apply: Normalize the language of feedback

- What's working?
- What's getting in the way?
- What support do we need?

Example: In one school system, leaders used short "clarity huddles" sessions where staff could openly name roadblocks. This led to less rework and boosted team morale.

3. Embed Adaptability

Why it matters: Rigid plans break under real-world pressure. Adaptive systems remain flexible while maintaining their core direction.

How to apply: Incorporate review points to adjust plans based on data and team feedback. Use visual tools, like digital Kanban boards, to track shifting priorities.

> Example: In Maya's community health project, teams conducted monthly "pivot reviews" to reallocate resources based on emerging needs. As a result, progress remained steady and relevant.

HARD-WON LESSON: JAMAL'S SHIFT TO EXECUTION RHYTHM

Jamal, the regional logistics manager, was spearheading a system overhaul. Initial progress was promising, but pressure caused the execution to crumble. Deadlines slipped away. Updates fell behind. Confidence plummeted.

Through **Work the Plan**, Jamal:

- Introduced biweekly "progress pulses" for each team to review top priorities, blockers, and next steps
- Created a shared execution dashboard that visualized real-time status and ownership
- Embedded adaptability by using client feedback to adjust priorities for each sprint

In just two months, delivery rates increased by 25%, and the staff reported feeling more confident and less overwhelmed in their roles. Jamal reflected, "We stopped trying to 'remember' the plan and started living it.".

THE EQUITY DIMENSION OF EXECUTION

Working the Plan isn't about enforcing compliance; it's about building systems that work for all brains. In the absence of clear execution rhythms, those with greater capacity, confidence, or informal knowledge take on more, while others fall behind—not due to lack of effort, but lack of access.

Leaders foster cognitive justice by embedding shared rhythms, feedback loops, and adaptive practices, cultivating a system of collective clarity, progress, and resilience.

≈ PAUSE. SPARK. ACT

Where is your team's execution stalling or losing momentum?

How can you establish regular rhythms— daily, weekly, monthly—to maintain momentum?

What safe channels can identify blockers before they escalate into crises?

How can you infuse adaptability into your current plan?

Feedback Loop

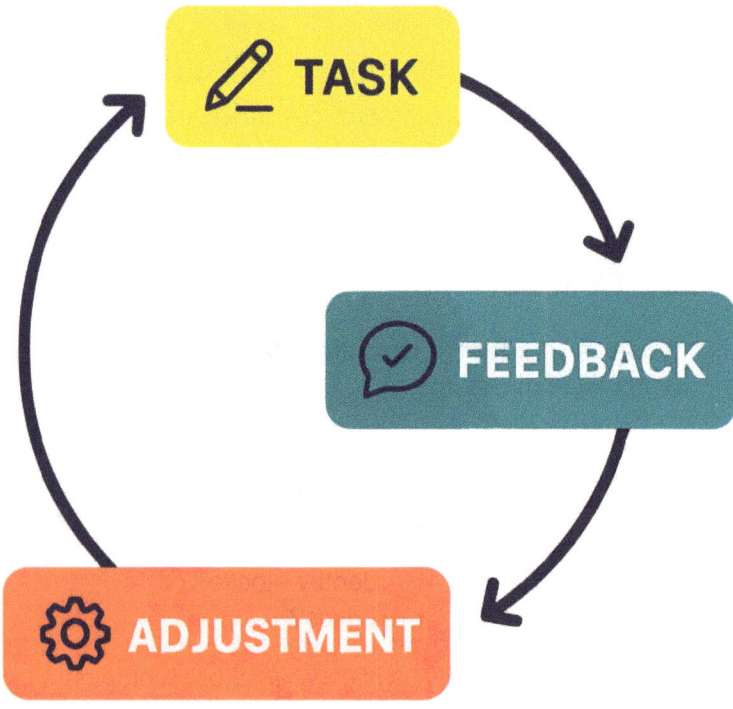

Figure: A Simple Loop That Keeps Execution Adaptive
Feedback isn't a detour—it's part of the work. This loop shows how teams can move from action to feedback to adjustment, then back to execution with more clarity. That's how momentum stays real, not rigid.

EF-WC-017: Learning Loop Tracker

F.L.O.W.™ Quadrant: Reflect & Recalibrate
EF Skills Supported: Metacognition, Strategic Adjustment, Identity Alignment
Best-Matched Strategy: Reflective Tracking, Feedback Integration
Format: Behavior → Feedback → Strategy → Adjustment Cycle Template

Purpose	To make EF development visible over time by tracking learning cycles and applying real-time adjustments.
When to Use This Tool	• After retrospectives or performance feedback • During leadership development or coaching cycles • To monitor growth and reinforce adaptive strategies
Step-by-Step Instructions	1. **Identify Learning Focus** Select a specific area of EF development or leadership practice. 2. **Document Observations** Capture behaviors, feedback received, and context. 3. **Plan Adjustments** Define new strategies or scaffolds to test. 4. **Track and Reflect** Note the outcomes, lessons learned, and adjustments for next iteration.
Template	Template | Date	Focus Area	Behavior Observed	Feedback	New Strategy	Notes
---	---	---	---	---	---	
Example Entry	Example Entry | Date	Focus Area	Behavior Observed	Feedback	New Strategy	Notes
---	---	---	---	---	---
2025-06-05	Follow-through	Delayed follow-up email	Missed deadline	Use task app reminders	Improved response time observed
2025-06-12	Meeting engagement	Passive participation	Low engagement	Prep speaking points	More active in next meeting	
Coaching Tip	Ask: "What pattern do you see emerging in your learning loop? Where can you adjust your approach for the next cycle?"

FLOW Execution Suite™ and its tools are part of the protected FLOW™ Executive Function System.
©2025. All rights reserved. For licensed use only.
Structure clarity. Support focus. Scale momentum.

Figure: A Simple Loop That Keeps Execution Adaptive
Feedback is part of the journey, not a detour. This loop demonstrates how teams transition from action to feedback, then to adjustment, and back to execution with greater clarity. That's how momentum remains dynamic, not rigid.

F.L.O.W.™ THE EQUITY-CENTERED COACHING FRAMEWORK

LOOKING AHEAD

WITH **WORK THE PLAN**, the F.L.O.W.™ loop completes its circle. F.L.O.W.™ empowers you to lead with focus, flexibility, and equity, transforming clarity into complexity and task design into structured action.

In the next chapter, we'll dive into integrating **F.L.O.W.™ across systems**—whether in coaching conversations, team structures, or organizational culture.

A system is only as strong as its sustaining rhythm.

"Flow happens when we align tasks with our strengths, energy, and purpose."

8
INTEGRATING F.L.O.W.™ ACROSS SYSTEMS

FROM PERSONAL PRACTICE TO ORGANIZATIONAL DESIGN

YOU'VE SEEN how F.L.O.W.™ enhances clarity, minimizes cognitive load, and promotes equity through its dynamic loop.

Find Your Focus → Level the Task → Organize for Action → Work the Plan

The true power of F.L.O.W.™ goes beyond individual leaders or isolated teams. It integrates cognitive clarity and adaptive momentum into the daily operations of teams, organizations, and entire sectors.

F.L.O.W.™ not only enhances productivity at various levels but also transforms how people work, connect, and lead.

Figure: Mapping the System to Make Clarity Scalable *One team's clarity isn't enough; system-wide clarity requires coordination. This moment demonstrates a team creating visibility at the organizational level by aligning tasks, roles, and rhythms across functions.*

THE RESEARCH BEHIND SYSTEMIC INTEGRATION

SUSTAINABLE CHANGE REQUIRES MORE than isolated actions. It comes from **aligned structures and cultures.**

Systems thinking (Senge, 1990) highlights that lasting change occurs when individuals, teams, and institutions align their mental models, routines, and feedback. F.L.O.W.™ provides a clear and adaptable framework that can be applied and strengthened in various contexts.

Organizational learning research (Argyris & Schön, 1978) shows that high-functioning systems incorporate **adaptive learning by** routinely reflecting, adjusting, and improving. F.L.O.W.™ supports this with continuous cycles and built-in reflection points.

The result? A framework that evolves from a personal habit into a **cultural norm.**

THREE LEVELS OF F.L.O.W.™ INTEGRATION

1. Individual Practice

Application: Leaders personally use F.L.O.W.™ to clarify priorities, break down tasks, align timelines, and maintain rhythms.
Example: A principal starts each week with a personal focus brief, then uses daily prompts to course-correct and manage cognitive load.
Impact: Greater clarity, reduced burnout, and lasting focus.

2. Team Rhythms

Application: Teams adopt F.L.O.W.™ in meetings, workflows, and communication norms. This includes shared Focus Briefs, visual task boards, aligned calendars, and regular check-ins.

Example: A nonprofit team holds weekly clarity huddles, shares updated task maps, and articulates blockers aloud.

Impact: Less ambiguity, stronger collaboration, and increased psychological safety.

3. System-Wide Design

Application: Organizations embed F.L.O.W.™ into their policies, performance systems, and leadership culture. This includes training, onboarding, coaching protocols, and adaptive planning structures.

Example: A multi-site healthcare network trains leaders in F.L.O.W.™, aligns quarterly goals with its phases, and tracks progress through shared dashboards.

Impact: A culture of clarity, higher retention, and more equitable execution across teams.

EQUITY AT THE SYSTEM LEVEL

Integrating F.L.O.W.™ at scale operationalizes **cognitive justice.**

It ensures that clarity, structure, and adaptability are not privileges reserved for those with positional power or insider knowledge. They become shared, accessible features of the environment. For neurodivergent leaders, BIPOC professionals, and those navigating complex social realities, this transformation is not only functional—it's liberating.

When teams normalize scaffolding and visibility, they no longer rely on individuals to self-correct for broken systems. Instead, the **system itself becomes sustainable.**

F.L.O.W.™ THE EQUITY-CENTERED COACHING FRAMEWORK

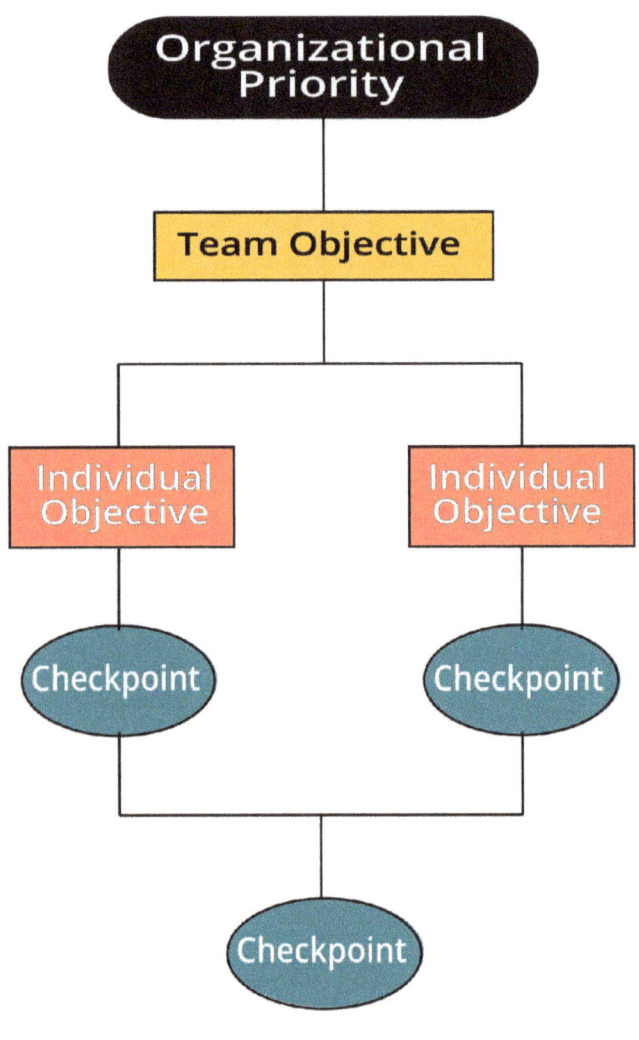

Figure: Cascading Clarity from Strategy to Execution *This map shows how one organizational priority flows down to team*

and individual objectives, with built-in checkpoints to make alignment visible and sustainable. When everyone sees how their work connects to the larger picture, clarity increases.

HARD-WON LESSON: SCALING F.L.O.W.™ IN A SCHOOL NETWORK

An urban school network was experiencing initiative fatigue and leadership burnout. Projects were started without coordination. Leaders juggled unclear priorities with minimal support.

By integrating F.L.O.W.™:

- Each school created a semester-long Focus Brief aligned with district goals
- Teams mapped tasks on leveled boards with assigned owners and due dates
- Weekly clarity huddles replaced reactive crisis meetings
- Leaders held adaptive review cycles every six weeks to refine plans in real time

The result was higher project completion rates, fewer decision bottlenecks, and a shared sense of direction. One principal said, For the first time, I don't have to fight for clarity. The system supports it.

PRACTICAL STEPS FOR INTEGRATION

1. **Start with a Pilot**
   - Choose a project or team to apply the full F.L.O.W.™ loop. Track progress and gather feedback. Let the success model ripple outward.
2. **Train and Model**
   - Provide leaders and coaches with F.L.O.W.™ tools, language, and templates, and consistently model them in meetings and planning.
3. **Embed in Systems**
   - Connect F.L.O.W.™ to goal-setting, performance reviews, meeting agendas, and professional development sessions. Create visual digital boards or dashboards that reinforce the loop.
4. **Reinforce with Reflection**
   - Use monthly or quarterly check-ins to evaluate how F.L.O.W.™ is performing. What is getting better? What should change? What new habits are forming?

≈ PAUSE. SPARK. ACT

At what level—personal, team, or system—can you begin applying F.L.O.W.™ today?

Which existing structures can you align with the F.L.O.W.™ loop to enhance clarity and resilience?

INTEGRATING F.L.O.W.™ ACROSS SYSTEMS

How will you implement cognitive scaffolding and adaptive leadership in your role?

LOOKING AHEAD

F.L.O.W.™ integration across systems establishes the foundation for sustainable leadership.

In the next chapter, we'll discuss how to **maintain F.L.O.W.™ over time,** transforming it from a set of tools into a lasting habit and cultural pillar.

Clarity is not just a practice; it's a way of working.

9
SUSTAINING F.L.O.W.™ OVER TIME

MAKING CLARITY A LEADERSHIP HABIT, NOT A ONE-TIME FIX

YOU'VE CREATED CLARITY. You've simplified complexity. You've established ownership and integrated execution processes. You've witnessed the transformation that F.L.O.W.™ produces when used intentionally.

But systems drift, stress returns, new projects pile up, and people leave. In those moments, even the best-designed structures can start to unravel.

Sustaining F.L.O.W.™ involves integrating it **into your habits, culture, and leadership identity, rather than just memorizing the steps.**

> Clarity is not a one-time achievement. It's a practice.

Figure: Making Progress Visible with a Habit Tracker *This is about recognizing patterns, not just checking boxes. A habit tracker helps maintain focus and reinforce small, strategic actions that build clarity, confidence, and consistency over time.*

THE PSYCHOLOGY OF HABIT AND DRIFT

Even the best leaders can experience drift. When stressed, our brains default to survival strategies—reactivity, urgency, and over-functioning. The prefrontal cortex, responsible for executive function, shuts down, leading to a loss of clarity (Diamond, 2013).

This is natural. But it's not inevitable.

Research on **habit formation** (Duhigg, 2012; Wood & Rünger,

2016) shows that lasting behavior change requires three elements:

1. **Cue** – A consistent trigger to start the behavior
2. **Routine** – A repeatable structure for the action
3. **Reward** – A meaningful benefit that reinforces the habit

F.L.O.W.™ can be incorporated into leadership practices using the same model.

HOW TO TURN F.L.O.W.™ INTO A HABIT LOOP

1. Cue: Anchor It to a Ritual

Connect each phase of F.L.O.W.™ to a current rhythm.

Examples:

- Start your week with a personal Focus Brief
- Open team meetings by leveling the current task
- End projects with a "Work the Plan" debrief and feedback loop

The key is consistency—use the same time, format, and tool each time. This automates the behavior until it becomes second nature.

2. Routine: Keep It Simple and Visible

Avoid overcomplicating the process. Use the same templates, boards, and language. Visibility reduces decision fatigue and supports shared ownership.

Tip: Set up a F.L.O.W.™ wall in your digital workspace or office. Update it weekly to reflect team priorities, task levels, and plans.

3. REWARD: NAME THE WINS

Acknowledge what is working. Celebrate when a Focus Brief provides clarity. Call out when a leveled task prevents overload. Recognize when a rhythm or feedback loop sustains momentum.

These "micro-wins" show that the system is functional and transformational.

THE THREE PILLARS OF SUSTAINING F.L.O.W.™

1. REINFORCE RHYTHMS AND RITUALS

Why It Matters: Clear and consistent rhythms lower cognitive load and enhance understanding. Even the best systems weaken under pressure without reinforcement.

How to Apply: Establish regular rhythms—weekly clarity meetings, monthly reviews, and quarterly F.L.O.W.™ reflections. Connect them to current organizational activities, such as staff meetings, project reviews, or leadership retreats.

Example: A community organization embedded a 10-

minute "priority round" into every leadership meeting, anchoring focus as a shared ritual.

2. Create Shared Ownership of Clarity

Why It Matters: Systems that rely on a few leaders are fragile. When clarity and focus are shared cultural norms, they become resilient.

How to Apply: Train all leaders in F.L.O.W.™ principles, not just senior staff. Use a common language among teams

> *Examples:* "Let's level this task," or "What's our focus this week?"

> Celebrate clarity wins publicly.

> Example: A school district created "Clarity Champions"—leaders at various levels who demonstrated F.L.O.W.™ practices and guided their peers, integrating the framework into daily routines.

3. Build Feedback into the System

Why It Matters: Feedback prevents systems from drifting. Feedback loops help practices adapt to real-world needs and support learning.

How to Apply: Create regular feedback cycles—such as surveys, reflection sessions, and coaching check-ins—to assess how F.L.O.W.™ is working. Use that data to adjust and maintain engagement.

> *Example:* A healthcare network used quarterly "clarity pulse" surveys to identify gaps, celebrate wins, and refine their use of F.L.O.W.™, keeping the practice alive over multiple years.

HARD-WON LESSON: WHEN THE SYSTEM SLIPS, RECOMMIT —DON'T RESTART

Three months after launching F.L.O.W.™, a senior team at a youth development nonprofit noticed its early momentum waning. The routines had lapsed. Focus briefs were not updated. Check-ins were inconsistent. The team began to fall back into old habits: reactive emails, late-night meetings, and unclear deliverables.

Initially, the leader's instinct was to "go back to the beginning" —retrain everyone, overhaul the process, start from scratch.

They paused and asked, **what part of the loop needs reinforcement, not reinvention?**

They conducted a quick feedback survey, showing that teams still believed in F.L.O.W.™; they just needed a **reset**, not a reboot. They resumed their weekly meetings, committed to shared task boards, and celebrated small wins to demonstrate progress.

Within weeks, energy and alignment returned.

One team member stated that the issue wasn't a system failure, but rather that we had forgotten to maintain it. Picking it up felt like returning to something that had always been ours.

The lesson? Systems drift. What matters is how we respond when they do.

≈ PAUSE. SPARK. ACT

> What cue can you use to incorporate F.L.O.W.™ into your weekly leadership routine?

> Which part of the loop do you usually skip when you are overwhelmed? How can you easily bring it back?

> How can you help your team make F.L.O.W.™ visible and shared, rather than just internal or individual?

> What reward would encourage you to maintain this habit?

THE EQUITY IMPERATIVE IN SUSTAINABILITY

Sustaining F.L.O.W.™ is both a productivity strategy and a practice of justice.

Systems that promote cognitive clarity and adaptive learning enable success for **everyone**, not just those who are well resourced, assertive, or neurotypical. When leaders establish structure, provide feedback, and ensure shared understanding, they lessen the cognitive load on those dealing with unspoken norms or systemic bias.

By maintaining flexible systems, we shift equity from a one-time effort to an ongoing practice.

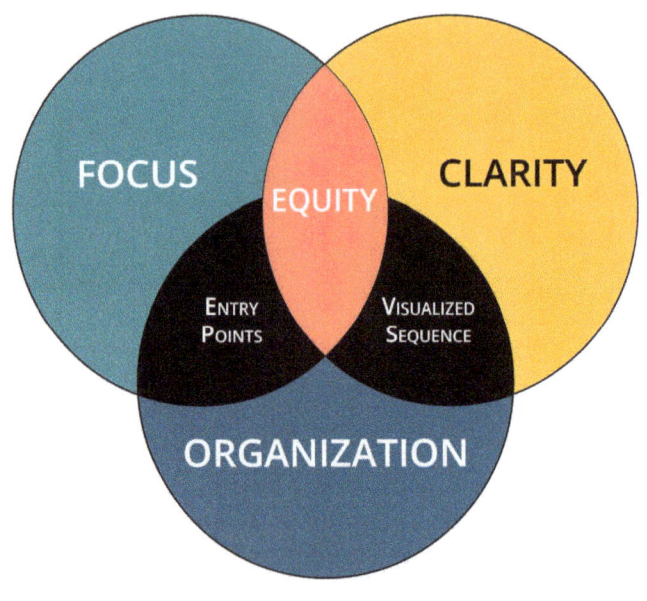

Figure: Equity Happens by Design *Equity becomes actionable where focus, clarity, and organization intersect. Entry points and visualized sequences make the overlap functional.*

THE CULTURE OF SUSTAINED CLARITY

When F.L.O.W.™ becomes the norm, the culture changes.

- People expect clarity—and know how to create it

- Teams rely on structure—not just memory or willpower
- Systems flex without collapsing under pressure
- Equity becomes operational, not aspirational

This happens gradually. It occurs gradually through repetition, modeling, and feedback.

Leaders who embrace F.L.O.W.™ prioritize **clarity as a core practice**, not just a planning phase.

LOOKING FORWARD

With sustained F.L.O.W.™, clarity evolves into more than just a tool; it transforms into a cultural foundation, a shared language, and a design principle for resilience, adaptability, and equity.

In the final section, we'll provide practical tools, templates, and quick-start guides to help you deepen your F.L.O.W.™ practice, ensuring that clarity is not just a fleeting win but a lasting shift.

Clarity isn't a sprint; it's a culture.

"Rest isn't a break from clarity—it's a catalyst for it."

CONCLUSION

A LEADERSHIP PRACTICE, NOT A ONE-TIME FIX

YOU'VE MOVED through the F.L.O.W.™ framework—spotlighting hidden cognitive overload, naming what matters most, reducing unnecessary complexity, organizing for action, and sustaining execution through rhythm and reflection.

But F.L.O.W.™ is more than a framework. It's a design language. A way of thinking, planning, and leading that centers clarity not as a luxury, but as a responsibility. It's a redefinition of what equity work looks like in action—and what human-centered leadership can actually feel like.

And this journey is just beginning.

From Knowing to Doing—From Doing to Modeling

Transformation doesn't come from new information alone. It comes from implementation, integration, and intention.

F.L.O.W.™ only reaches its potential when it becomes embedded in how we lead, coach, plan, and support others.

This is not a one-time reset. It's a system shift that unfolds in cycles, conversations, and courageous decisions.

THIS MATTERS NOW MORE THAN EVER

In a culture where speed often outruns strategy and urgency masquerades as effectiveness, we are asked to lead through the noise and produce clarity in the absence of it. That strain falls hardest on those already managing invisible labor, systemic barriers, or divergent cognitive needs.

Leaders now face a choice:

- Keep playing organizational whack-a-mole—chasing tasks, reacting to fires, and watching your people erode under ambiguity.
- Or commit to intentional clarity—building systems where equity isn't aspirational, but accessible.

This isn't about working harder.

It's about leading smarter, designing better, and reclaiming clarity as a collective asset.

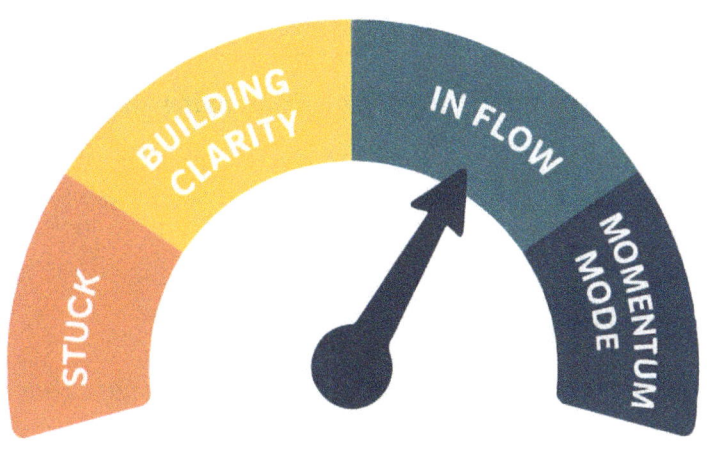

Figure: The Momentum Meter *This visual illustrates the feeling of momentum in practice, starting from feeling stuck, to gaining clarity, to flowing, and finally reaching full momentum. It serves as a shared language for teams to identify their situations and the support they may need.*

YOUR ROLE AS A LEADER OF CLARITY

Regardless of whether you're an executive, coach, team leader, or educator, you can:

- **Model F.L.O.W.™** – Show what clarity, structure, and rhythm look like in action
- **Create safe spaces for reflection** – Where blockers can surface and learning can take root
- **Align systems with human brains** – Design environments where clarity isn't a perk, but a norm

- **Anchor equity in practice** – Dismantle hidden labor, reduce ambiguity, and make momentum accessible to all

The role of a clarity-centered leader isn't to have all the answers. It's to design environments where the answers can emerge.

A PERSONAL REFLECTION

I wrote this book because I have experienced systems that demanded clarity from me without **providing it, forcing me** to support others while managing an unseen cognitive burden.

I understand the challenge of managing demands without a structure. I have experienced the burden of remaining "on" in a system that values reaction over reflection.

I've also witnessed the effects of changing the narrative. By slowing down. By scaffolding our thinking and designing for focus, equity, and resilience.

> We don't just survive the work—we **transform it.**

I invite you to take this step with me.

CONCLUSION

YOUR CALL TO ACTION

As you close this book, I challenge you to:

1. **Choose One Practice**
   - Choose one F.L.O.W.™ tool or habit to implement this week. Start small: share a Focus Brief, reframe a task, and establish a feedback loop.
2. **Engage a Partner**
   - Share your commitment with a colleague, coach, or teammate. Clarity is contagious.
3. **Track Your Progress**
   - Use the tools in this book—reflection prompts, feedback check-ins, and clarity audits—to measure momentum over time.
4. **Model the Way**
   - Be a leader who communicates clearly, confronts obstacles boldly, and **prioritizes equity** in both words and systems.

A FINAL WORD

Clarity is more than a leadership trait.

It's a form of justice. A countercultural practice in systems built for overwhelm.

With F.L.O.W.™, you're not just managing tasks. You're shaping culture, scaffolding equity, and designing with humanity at the core.

This is the first step. The next chapters—tools, templates, and transformational conversations—are still to come.

And you're ready.

Let's keep going.

PRACTICAL TOOLS & TEMPLATES FOR F.L.O.W.™

FROM REFLECTION TO ACTION

The power of F.L.O.W.™ lies not just in understanding its principles but also in applying them systematically. The following tools and templates provide a clear pathway from theory to practice, integrating executive skills development, personalized coaching, and cognitive flow design. These resources are designed for leaders, coaches, educators, and individuals seeking sustainable clarity and momentum.

The F.L.O.W.™ Toolkit

The F.L.O.W.™ framework is more than a concept; it's a practice. These tools help you apply each stage of F.L.O.W.™ in real time, with clarity and confidence.

F.L.O.W.™ THE EQUITY-CENTERED COACHING FRAMEWORK

FIND YOUR FOCUS (F)

This section provides tools to help you clarify your priorities and align your focus with what matters most. These tools anchor your attention and reduce cognitive clutter.

1. EF-WC-001: Focus Brief

    Purpose: Clarifies priorities and aligns actions with immediate goals.
    How to Use: Use this brief at the start of each week or project to establish a clear focus and reduce mental clutter.

2. EF-WC-002: Pause + Reprioritize Pulse

    Purpose: Helps reset priorities when overwhelmed.
    How to Use: Use to regain clarity during moments of overload and prioritize effectively.

LEVEL THE TASK (L)

These tools help you break complex tasks down into manageable steps. They reduce overload, align collaboration, and ensure clarity in responsibilities and processes.

3. EF-WC-003: Task Clarity Brief

    Purpose: Breaks down complex tasks into actionable steps, reducing overload.
    How to Use: This guide is useful when starting new projects, tackling overwhelming tasks, or delegating effectively.

4. EF-WC-005: Collaboration Compass

    Purpose: Align team efforts and clarify collaboration norms.
    How to Use: Use this to establish shared norms and expectations for collaboration.

5. EF-WC-006: Role Mapping Template

    Purpose: Clarifies roles and responsibilities for Organize for Action.
    How to Use: Use it to map out responsibilities and ensure everyone knows their part.

ORGANIZE FOR ACTION (O)

These tools prepare your environment, systems, and schedules for focused, uninterrupted progress.

6. EF-WC-028: Organizational Clarity Map

    Purpose: Cascades priorities across teams and aligns actions.
    How to Use: Use this tool to visualize and communicate team priorities, ensuring alignment.

7. EF-WC-029: Project Rhythm Systems

    Purpose: To help sequence projects and actions for sustainable clarity.
    How to Use: Structure project phases and align execution across teams.

8. EF-WC-030: Organizational Cadence Calendar

    Purpose: Embeds clarity and rhythm into systems.
    How to Use: Establish recurring schedules and touchpoints for sustained clarity.

PRACTICAL TOOLS & TEMPLATES FOR F.L.O.W.™

WORK THE PLAN (W)

Tools in this section help you sustain momentum, reflect on progress, and adapt strategies for continuous improvement. They ensure that your plans translate into intentional and effective action.

9. EF-WC-014: Leader's Guide to EF Strategy Use

    Purpose: Equip leaders to tailor EF strategies for their teams.
    How to Use: Align executive function strategies with individual and team strengths.

10. EF-WC-015: Leader's Interpretation Tool

    Purpose: Translates feedback into clear, actionable steps.
    How to Use: Turn team or individual feedback into practical action plans.

11. EF-WC-017: Learning Loop Tracker

    Purpose: Enables continuous improvement and reflection.
    How to Use: Use to reflect on progress, adapt strategies, and sustain momentum.

Access the Full Toolkit Online

For additional tools, templates, and resources—including those referenced in this book—visit the F.L.O.W. Execution Suite™ online hub. The digital resources provide an expanded set of tools to support your leadership journey, including downloadable templates and interactive guides.

Explore the full suite at: www.chanjecollective.com

EF-WC-001: Focus Brief

F.L.O.W.™ Quadrant: F – Find Your Focus
EF Skills Supported: Planning, Attention, Self-Monitoring
Best-Matched Strategy: Goal Chunking, Visual Anchoring
Format: Fillable Brief + Team-Facing Usage Guide

Purpose	To reduce overwhelm and sharpen task alignment by clearly defining the one top priority, aligned goals, and visible actions.
When to Use This Tool	<ul><li>Weekly team planning or kickoff</li><li>New project or sprint launch</li><li>When priorities feel scattered or reactive</li></ul>
Step-by-Step Instructions	1. **Name the Priority** One main objective. Use a behavior-focused action (e.g., "Draft onboarding guide"). 2. **Set 3 Meaningful Goals** ○ Milestone-style goals are aligned with the priority. ○ Use verbs like deliver, finalize, and align. 3. **List 5 Visible Tasks** ○ Concrete steps you can see or check off. ○ Avoid vague actions like "think about..." 4. **Check for Cognitive Fit** Ask: Is this visible? Reasonable? Sequenced? 5. **Anchor in Rhythm** ○ Share in the team space ○ Refer to it in weekly standups or 1:1s
Template	→ **This Week's Priority:** [One behavioral objective] → **3 Supporting Goals:** → **5 Visible Tasks:** → **Owner:** → **Check-in Point:**
Coaching Tip	Ask: "What's your one thing right now? What would be enough to say it's moving?"

FLOW Execution Suite™ and its tools are part of the protected FLOW™ Executive Function System.
©2025. All rights reserved. For licensed use only.
Structure clarity. Support focus. Scale momentum.

EF-WC-002: Pause + Reprioritize Pulse

F.L.O.W.™ Quadrant: F – Find Your Focus
EF Skills Supported: Self-Regulation, Inhibition
Best-Matched Strategy: Delay Techniques, Reflective Prompting
Format: Guided Ritual + Fillable Template

Purpose	To disrupt reactivity, surface overload, and reset priorities through a shared, cognitively grounded pause.
When to Use This Tool	• Visible overload or urgency loops • Mid-sprint, post-change, or pre-retro • When work feels performative or chaotic

Step-by-Step Instructions	1. **Pause Intentionally** "Let's pause before we keep going—just for a few minutes."
	2. **Run a Pulse Prompt**
	Choose 1–2:
	   ◦ What were we actually trying to move forward?
	   ◦ What's being done out of momentum, not purpose?
	   ◦ What task no longer makes sense?
	   ◦ What can we delay or drop?
	3. **Reprioritize Collectively**
	   ◦ Name one top priority
	   ◦ Delay, cancel, or sequence out misaligned tasks
	   ◦ Mark changes visibly
	4. **Reset the Rhythm**
	   ◦ Reshare priorities in a visible workspace
	   ◦ Name the next check-in clearly

Template	➔ Date: ➔ Who is pausing (team/individual): ➔ Signal (what prompted pause): ➔ Pulse Prompts Used: ➔ Removed or Delayed: ➔ New Top Priority: ➔ Next Check-In:
Coaching Tip	Reactivity is not a failure—it's a signal. Normalize pause as a strategy, not an interruption.

FLOW Execution Suite™ and its tools are part of the protected FLOW™ Executive Function System.
©2025. All rights reserved. For licensed use only.
Structure clarity. Support focus. Scale momentum.

EF-WC-003: Task Clarity Brief

F.L.O.W.™ Quadrant: L – Level the Task
EF Skills Supported: Task Initiation, Planning, Working Memory
Best-Matched Strategy: Behavioral Activation, Sequencing, Externalization
Format: Fillable Brief + Team-Facing Usage Guide

Purpose	Break down vague or cognitively heavy tasks into clear, startable steps. It prevents stalling, fog, and ambiguity.
When to Use This Tool	<ul><li>Before assigning cognitively heavy tasks</li><li>When someone delays starting</li><li>During kickoff or sprint planning</li><li>When mental fog is high</li></ul>

Step-by-Step Instructions	1. **Write the Task in Behavioral Language**
	e.g., "Draft curriculum flow options," not "Figure out the curriculum."
	2. **Define What 'Start' Looks Like**
	Ask: "What would I see you doing if you started?"
	3. **Break the Task into 3–5 Steps**
	   ◦ Visible, sequenced, and grounded in action.
	4. **Add Scaffolds**
	Share examples, templates, or visuals that guide the work.
	5. **Confirm Ownership and Check-In**
	   ◦ Clarify who owns it and when it will be revisited.

Template	→ Task: [Behavioral description] → What counts as "starting"? [Describe first action] → Steps to Complete: → Links, Docs, or Examples Provided: [Paste or attach] → Owner: → Next Check-In:
Coaching Tip	"What would count as starting?" Use this when a task feels mentally stuck or delayed.

FLOW Execution Suite™ and its tools are part of the protected FLOW™ Executive Function System.
©2025. All rights reserved. For licensed use only.
Structure clarity. Support focus. Scale momentum.

EF-WC-005: Collaboration Compass

F.L.O.W.™ Quadrant: O – Organize for Action
EF Skills Supported: Organization, Working Memory, Self-Regulation
Best-Matched Strategy: Shared Tracking, Role Anchoring, Externalization
Format: Team Alignment Worksheet + Working Agreement Template

Purpose	Align collaborators before action. Prevents misfires, confusion, and floating ownership.
When to Use This Tool	<ul><li>Before cross-functional work begins</li><li>When multiple owners are involved</li><li>To reset clarity on joint deliverables</li><li>When "I thought you were doing that" is common</li></ul>

Step-by-Step Instructions	1. **Name the Collaboration**
	Describe it clearly and behaviorally.
	2. **Define Compass Roles**
	    ○ Driver
	    ○ Support
	    ○ Decision Input
	    ○ Visibility
	3. **Identify the Workspace**
	Link to Notion, slide, board, etc.
	4. **Set Support Rhythm**
	Weekly sync, async comment, etc.
	5. **Post It Visibly**
	Add to the board, Slack, or project doc.

Template	**Collaboration Name:** [Describe it clearly and behaviorally] **Compass Roles:** → **Driver:** [Name of person responsible] → **Support:** [Names of people providing support] → **Decision Input:** [Names or teams providing input] → **Visibility:** [Names or teams who need to be informed] → **Workspace:** [Link to collaboration space] → **Check-In Rhythm:** [Frequency and method of check-in] → **Notes or Boundaries:** [Any additional relevant information]
Coaching Tip	Misalignment is structural, not personal. Use this before the work—not after the fire.

EF-WC-006: Role Mapping Template

F.L.O.W.™ Quadrant: O – Organize for Action
EF Skills Supported: Organization, Planning
Best-Matched Strategy: Role Clarity, Visual Anchoring
Format: Shared Ownership Map + Revisit Rhythm Prompt

Purpose	Make ownership, support, and check-ins visible. It prevents confusion and uneven accountability.
When to Use This Tool	<ul><li>Launching new initiatives</li><li>Coordinating cross-team work</li><li>When ownership is vague or overlapping</li><li>When support or follow-through is inconsistent</li></ul>
Step-by-Step Instructions	1. **Name the Initiative or Team** 2. **Map Lead Ownership** Define key deliverables and owners. 3. **Document Support + Check-Ins** 4. **Add Workspace Links** Paste shared folders, Notion pages, etc. 5. **Use as Live Artifact** Bring to meetings and update regularly.
Template	**Initiative Name:** **Ownership Map:** | Area / Deliverable	Lead Owner	Support Roles	Check-In Rhythm	Workspace Link
---	---	---	---	---
					  Review Rhythm: [Monthly, sprintly, etc.] **Notes:** [Where is support missing or unclear?]
Coaching Tip	Don't just name roles—show them. Visibility closes the loop.

FLOW Execution Suite™ and its tools are part of the protected FLOW™ Executive Function System.
©2025. All rights reserved. For licensed use only.
Structure clarity. Support focus. Scale momentum.

EF-WC-014: Leader's Guide to EF Strategy Use

F.L.O.W.™ Quadrant: All
EF Skills Supported: All Domains
Best-Matched Strategy: Insight-to-Structure Loop, Cognitive Coaching
Format: Step-by-Step Guide + Tool Matching Table

Purpose	Help leaders translate EF friction into tool-based support. Create momentum through clarity—not more effort.
When to Use This Tool	<ul><li>After survey, feedback, or observed strain</li><li>During planning, retros, or coaching</li><li>To design cognitively safer systems</li></ul>
Step-by-Step Instructions	**Step 1: Spot the Signal** <ul><li>"We're stuck" → Initiation</li><li>"No clarity" → Planning</li><li>"Things get dropped" → Working Memory</li><li>"Reactivity" → Inhibition</li></ul>**Step 2: Identify the EF Skill** Use surveys or pattern tables. **Step 3: Filter the Tool Index** Match EF domain or FLOW quadrant. **Step 4: Choose Structural Tool**<ul><li>Initiation → Task Brief</li><li>Monitoring → EF Pulse</li><li>Planning → Focus Brief</li><li>Collaboration → Role Map</li></ul>**Step 5: Scaffold, Don't Shame** "This supports your thinking—not your effort." **Step 6: Embed + Normalize** Put tools in meetings, threads, and cycles—not just links.
Template	Quick EF Pattern Table | Signal	EF Domain	Tool
---	---	---
Delay	Initiation	Task Clarity Brief
Chaos	Planning	Focus Brief
Drops	Memory	Rhythm Map
Reactivity	Inhibition	Pause + Pulse
Unclear roles	Org	Role Mapping	
Coaching Tip	You're not correcting behavior—you're redesigning conditions. Lead through structure, not pressure.

FLOW Execution Suite™ and its tools are part of the protected FLOW™ Executive Function System.
©2025. All rights reserved. For licensed use only.
Structure clarity. Support focus. Scale momentum.

EF-WC-015: Leader's Interpretation Tool

F.L.O.W.™ Quadrants: All
EF Skills Supported: Pattern Recognition, Metacognition, Planning
Best-Matched Strategy: EF Insight Loop + Structural Response
Format: Score-to-Tool Matrix + Action Tracker

Purpose	Help leaders translate EF friction into structural support. Move from signal to solution—without guessing.
When to Use This Tool	• After EF Pulse or Structural Survey • During team retro or 1:1s • After tension, delay, or patterning issues • As part of planning cycles

Step-by-Step Instructions	1. **Collect Signal Data**
	From surveys, notes, behavior
	2. **Find EF Domain**
	Match signal to the EF skill (see matrix)
	3. **Use Tool Matrix**
	Choose tool(s) that support the friction
	4. **Log the Response**
	  ○ What was selected
	  ○ Where it lives
	  ○ When you'll check in
	5. **Revisit in 30–60 Days**
	Use follow-up to measure shift

Template	Response Tracker → Team/Project: → EF Domain: → Signal or Score: → Tool Chosen: → Where It Lives: → Check-In Date:

EF Interpretation Matrix

EF Skill	Signal	Tool Match	Notes
Planning	Fog, unclear next	Focus Brief, Flow Cycle	Re-sequence
Initiation	Delays, freeze	Task Brief, Delegation	Start clarity
Memory	Drop-offs	Rhythm Map, Tracker	Visibility
Organization	Can't find tools/info	Role Map, Compass	Restructure workspace
Regulation	Reactivity	Pause + Pulse, Anchors	Add containment
Inhibition	Overcommits	Handoff Norm, Anchors	Delay prompts
Monitoring	"Off track"	EF Pulse, Review	Reflective rhythm
Flexibility	Can't pivot	Think Aloud, Compass	Model aloud
Attention	Scattered	Focus Brief, Weekly Sync	Weekly reset

Coaching Tip	This tool answers: "Now what?" It makes EF feedback **actionable and structural.**

FLOW Execution Suite™ and its tools are part of the protected FLOW™ Executive Function System.
©2025. All rights reserved. For licensed use only.
Structure clarity. Support focus. Scale momentum.

EF-WC-017: Learning Loop Tracker

F.L.O.W.™ Quadrant: Reflect & Recalibrate
EF Skills Supported: Metacognition, Strategic Adjustment, Identity Alignment
Best-Matched Strategy: Reflective Tracking, Feedback Integration
Format: Behavior → Feedback → Strategy → Adjustment Cycle Template

Purpose	To make EF development visible over time by tracking learning cycles and applying real-time adjustments.
When to Use This Tool	<ul><li>After retrospectives or performance feedback</li><li>During leadership development or coaching cycles</li><li>To monitor growth and reinforce adaptive strategies</li></ul>
Step-by-Step Instructions	1. **Identify Learning Focus** Select a specific area of EF development or leadership practice. 2. **Document Observations** Capture behaviors, feedback received, and context. 3. **Plan Adjustments** Define new strategies or scaffolds to test. 4. **Track and Reflect** Note the outcomes, lessons learned, and adjustments for next iteration.
Template	Template | Date	Focus Area	Behavior Observed	Feedback	New Strategy	Notes
---	---	---	---	---	---
Example Entry	Example Entry | Date	Focus Area	Behavior Observed	Feedback	New Strategy	Notes
---	---	---	---	---	---
2025-06-05	Follow-through	Delayed follow-up email	Missed deadline	Use task app reminders	Improved response time observed
2025-06-12	Meeting engagement	Passive participation	Low engagement	Prep speaking points	More active in next meeting	
Coaching Tip	Ask: "What pattern do you see emerging in your learning loop? Where can you adjust your approach for the next cycle?"

FLOW Execution Suite™ and its tools are part of the protected FLOW™ Executive Function System.
©2025. All rights reserved. For licensed use only.
Structure clarity. Support focus. Scale momentum.

EF-WC-028: Organizational Clarity Map

F.L.O.W.™ Quadrant: O – Organize for Action
EF Skills Supported: Strategic Planning, Distributed Cognition, System Alignment
Best-Matched Strategy: Clarity Mapping, Priority Cascading
Format: Visual Clarity Map + Table Matrix (Can be created as a diagram or in table format for clarity at multiple levels.)

Purpose	To scale individual task clarity into an organization-wide alignment map that clarifies priorities, ownership, and execution rhythm.
When to Use This Tool	<ul><li>During strategic planning or quarterly alignment</li><li>In large-scale projects with multiple teams</li><li>When clarity breaks down across levels</li></ul>
Step-by-Step Instructions	1. **Identify Top-Level Priorities** Determine the organization's key focus areas. 2. **Map Clarity Cascades** Show how priorities break into team-level and individual objectives. 3. **Assign Ownership & Checkpoints** Document owners, timelines, and rhythm for review. 4. **Communicate the Map** Share visual clarity maps across teams to support alignment.
Template	**Template** | Priority	Team Objective	Owner	Checkpoint
---	---	---	---
Example Entry	**Example Entry** | Priority	Team Objective	Owner	Checkpoint
---	---	---	---
Improve Client Engagement	Develop new onboarding workflow	Ops Manager	Q3 Review
Enhance Product Quality	Implement QC dashboards	QA Lead	Monthly	
Coaching Tip	Ask: "Does everyone know how their work connects to the bigger picture? Where can we increase clarity?"

FLOW Execution Suite™ and its tools are part of the protected FLOW™ Executive Function System.
©2025. All rights reserved. For licensed use only.
Structure clarity. Support focus. Scale momentum.

EF-WC-029: Project Rhythm Systems

F.L.O.W.™ Quadrant: W – Work the Plan
EF Skills Supported: Sequencing, Follow-Through, Coordination
Best-Matched Strategy: Phased Planning, Ownership Mapping
Format: Phased Plan Template + Calendar Integration (can be visual or table-based for clarity)

Purpose	To translate task sequencing into full project management rhythms, supporting clear coordination and adaptive cycles.
When to Use This Tool	<ul><li>For complex, cross-team initiatives</li><li>When clarity is needed across project phases</li><li>During planning cycles or retrospectives</li></ul>
Step-by-Step Instructions	1. **Map Project Phases** Break the project into clear stages (e.g., planning, development, delivery). 2. **Assign Owners and Timelines** Document who owns each phase, and its deadlines. 3. **Set Check-In and Adjustment Points** Establish points for team reviews and recalibration. 4. **Integrate into Calendars** Add milestones and check-ins to shared calendars for visibility.
Template	**Template** | Phase	Task/Objective	Owner	Timeline
---	---	---	---
Planning	Define project scope	Project Lead	Q1
Development	Build core features	Dev Team	Q2
Delivery	Deploy and train	Ops Lead	Q3
Review	Collect feedback	PM Team	Q4	
Example Entry	**Example Entry** | Phase	Task/Objective	Owner	Timeline
---	---	---	---
Initiation	Kickoff meeting	PM Lead	July 2025
Development	Draft product specs	Engineering	Aug 2025
Launch	Release product	Ops Lead	Oct 2025
Post-Launch	Customer feedback	Support	Nov 2025	
Coaching Tip	Ask: "Where might this project lose momentum? How can we maintain a clear rhythm?"

FLOW Execution Suite™ and its tools are part of the protected FLOW™ Executive Function System.
©2025. All rights reserved. For licensed use only.
Structure clarity. Support focus. Scale momentum.

EF-WC-030: Organizational Cadence Calendar

F.L.O.W.™ Quadrant: W – Work the Plan
EF Skills Supported: Follow-Through, Habit Formation, Coordination
Best-Matched Strategy: Scaled Checkback, Habit Anchoring
Format: Calendar Template + Rhythm Guide

Purpose	To embed a consistent review and recalibration rhythm across the organization, sustaining clarity and momentum.
When to Use This Tool	<ul><li>During quarterly or monthly planning cycles</li><li>During periods of organizational change</li><li>To establish consistency in follow-through across teams</li></ul>
Step-by-Step Instructions	1. **Map Key Review Points** Identify recurring check-ins (e.g., monthly reviews, quarterly strategy sessions). 2. **Schedule Events and Assign Owners** Document dates, responsible leads, and focus areas. 3. **Communicate Across Teams** Share the cadence calendar to ensure shared understanding and commitment. 4. **Monitor and Adjust** Track adherence to the rhythm and adapt as needed for effectiveness.
Template Example Entry	**Template** | Date | Event | Owner | Notes | |---|---|---|---| | | | | | **Example Entry** | Date | Event | Owner | Notes | |---|---|---|---| | 2025-07-01 | Monthly Strategy Sync | Leadership Team | Review Q3 goals and blockers | | 2025-07-15 | Mid-Month Progress Check | Project Leads | Identify friction points | | 2025-07-31 | End-of-Month Review | All Teams | Reflect on wins and adjustments |
Coaching Tip	Ask: "What's one cadence element we can add to increase clarity and accountability?"

FLOW Execution Suite™ and its tools are part of the protected FLOW™ Executive Function System.
©2025. All rights reserved. For licensed use only.
Structure clarity. Support focus. Scale momentum.

GLOSSARY OF F.L.O.W.™ TERMS

Clarity Anchor
The specific question, visual, or structure that helps someone pause, refocus, and move forward with intention. Every phase of F.L.O.W.™ offers one.

Cognitive Justice
The idea that all ways of thinking and processing—especially those shaped by race, disability, language, or culture—deserve equal value and structural support. In F.L.O.W.™, this means designing tools and systems that don't just accommodate differences but are *built* for them.

Cognitive Scaffolding
Structures—such as checklists, briefs, or mapped tasks—that reduce the mental load required to start, sequence, or complete work. Not a crutch, but a clarity multiplier.

Executive Function (EF)
The brain's self-management system includes skills such as planning, focus, impulse control, and working memory. F.L.O.W.™ tools are designed to support and externalize these functions.

Focus Brief
A weekly tool that focuses attention on one clear priority, three aligned goals, and five visible tasks. Designed to combat overwhelm with intentional clarity.

Friction
The invisible resistance that slows down execution is caused by unclear tasks, misaligned roles, unspoken expectations, or missing scaffolds. F.L.O.W.™ doesn't just name friction; it builds systems that reduce it.

Learning Loop
A feedback cycle: Task → Feedback → Adjustment. Helps teams move from trial to insight to improved execution without overcorrection.

Masking Trap
The hidden effort of appearing fine while managing a heavy executive load. Often invisible, especially in high-performing leaders.

Momentum Meter
A visual metaphor that helps teams identify their current state: stuck, building

clarity, in flow, or in momentum mode. Not diagnostic—just a shared language for moving forward.

Organizational Clarity Map

A flow visual shows how one major priority cascades to team and individual objectives, making alignment visible across levels.

Rhythm Map

A tool that outlines the "when" of work: check-ins, handoffs, and syncs. Helps teams transform routines into predictable, visible systems.

Role Mapping

A visibility tool that identifies drivers, support roles, rhythms, and links for key work areas—ensuring accountability is shared and follow-through is easier.

Task Clarity

Breaking a task into visible, actionable steps makes it manageable. A vague request becomes a concrete sequence. It's not simplification; it's translation.

Tool Brief

A short planning tool embedded within chapters that translates cognitive strategies into repeatable workflows.

BIBLIOGRAPHY

Argyris, C., & Schön, D. A. (1978). *Organizational learning: A theory of action perspective.* Addison-Wesley.

Barkley, R. A. (2012). *Executive functions: What they are, how they work, and why they evolved.* Guilford Press.

Csikszentmihalyi, M. (1990). *Flow: The psychology of optimal experience.* Harper & Row.

Diamond, A. (2013). Executive functions. *Annual Review of Psychology, 64*(1), 135–168. https://doi.org/10.1146/annurev-psych-113011-143750

Duhigg, C. (2012). *The power of habit: Why we do what we do in life and business.* Random House.

Edmondson, A. (1999). Psychological safety and learning behavior in work teams. *Administrative Science Quarterly, 44*(2), 350–383. https://doi.org/10.2307/2666999

Fixsen, D. L., Naoom, S. F., Blase, K. A., Friedman, R. M., & Wallace, F. (2005). *Implementation research: A synthesis of the literature* (FMHI Publication No. 231). University of South Florida, Louis de la Parte Florida Mental Health Institute, National Implementation Research Network.

Gollwitzer, P. M. (1999). Implementation intentions: Strong effects of simple plans. *American Psychologist, 54*(7), 493–503. https://doi.org/10.1037/0003-066X.54.7.493

Heifetz, R., & Linsky, M. (2002). *Leadership on the line: Staying alive through the dangers of leading.* Harvard Business School Press.

Meadows, D. H. (2008). *Thinking in systems: A primer.* Chelsea Green Publishing.

Senge, P. M. (1990). *The fifth discipline: The art and practice of the learning organization.* Doubleday/Currency.

Sweller, J. (1988). Cognitive load during problem solving: Effects on learning. *Cognitive Science, 12*(2), 257–285. https://doi.org/10.1207/s15516709cog1202_4

Tan, S. L., Ouyang, Y., & Li, H. (2022). Executive function and employee engagement: The mediating role of psychological well-being. *Frontiers in Psychology, 13,* Article 845196. https://doi.org/10.3389/fpsyg.2022.845196

Wood, W., & Neal, D. T. (2007). A new look at habits and the habit-goal interface. *Psychological Review, 114*(4), 843–863. https://doi.org/10.1037/0033-295X.114.4.843

ABOUT THE AUTHOR

Dr. Reba Clarke-Wedderburn is a visionary educator, leadership coach, and equity strategist committed to transforming how organizations think, work, and thrive. With over twenty years of experience in K-12, higher education, instructional design, and organizational change, she has established herself as a fierce advocate for cognitive equity and clarity-driven leadership.

As founder of **The Chanje Collective,** Dr. Clarke-Wedderburn leverages her coaching, curriculum development, and professional learning expertise to empower mission-driven organizations. She empowers leaders to create structures that respect diverse cognitive needs and operational realities. Her work transcends teaching strategies; it designs environments where clarity, resilience, and inclusion are essentials, not extras.

Dr. Clarke-Wedderburn earned a professional doctorate in Learning Organizations and Strategic Change from Lipscomb University, a Master's degree in Instructional Leadership, and a Bachelor's degree in Exceptional Education. Her approach fuses evidence-based insights from cognitive science, equity-centered coaching frameworks, and personal experiences at the complex intersections of race, neurodivergence, and leadership.

Dr. Clarke-Wedderburn has shaped publications such as *Centering Our Voices: The Brilliance, Persistence, and Significance of Black Women Educators* and spearheaded professional learning initiatives. Her work has revolutionized classrooms, coaching practices, and leadership teams nationwide.

Beyond consulting and designing scalable systems for clarity and momentum, she champions inclusive practices that illuminate brilliance, particularly for those frequently marginalized by traditional structures.

- threads.net/@achanjecoach
- linkedin.com/in/rclarkew
- bsky.app/profile/chanjecollective.bsky.social
- patreon.com/chanje

www.ingramcontent.com/pod-product-compliance
Lightning Source LLC
Chambersburg PA
CBHW071213160426
43196CB00011B/2290